AUSTRALIAN WRITERS
PATRICK WHITE

AUSTRALIAN WRITERS

The *Australian Writers* series examines in succinct form the lives and works of Australia's major writers. This authoritative series, under the General Editorship of Chris Wallace-Crabbe, will become essential reading for all who are seriously interested in Australian literature. *Australian Writers* is a timely and expansive successor to Oxford's earlier *Australian Writers and Their Work* series, and takes account of new cultural formations and developments in literary theory. At the same time, these provoking books contain elements of biography and are aimed at the intelligent general reader.

General Editor
Chris Wallace-Crabbe is the holder of a Personal Chair at the University of Melbourne.
Educated at Melbourne and Yale Universities, he has an international reputation as a poet. Recent books include *For Crying out Loud*, a collection of poems, and *Falling into Language*, a collection of critical essays. In 1987–88 he held the Visiting Chair of Australian Studies at Harvard.

OXFORD

AUSTRALIAN WRITERS

PATRICK WHITE

SIMON DURING

Melbourne

OXFORD UNIVERSITY PRESS

Oxford   Auckland   New York

OXFORD UNIVERSITY PRESS AUSTRALIA

Oxford New York
Athens Auckland Bangkok Bombay
Calcutta Cape Town Dar es Salaam Delhi
Florence Hong Kong Istanbul Karachi
Kuala Lumpur Madras Madrid Melbourne
Mexico City Nairobi Paris Singapore
Taipei Tokyo Toronto

and associated companies in
Berlin Ibadan

OXFORD is a trade mark of Oxford University Press

© Simon During 1996
First published 1996

National Library of Australia
Cataloguing-in-Publication data

During, Simon, 1950–
  Patrick White

  Bibliography.
  ISBN 0 19 553497 2

  1. White, Patrick, 1912–1990 — Criticism and interpretation.
  I. Title. (Series: Australian Writers (Melbourne, Vic.)).

A823.3

Printed by Australian Print Group
Published by Oxford University Press,
253 Normanby Road, South Melbourne, Australia

CONTENTS

A Note on Texts and Abbreviations

Page references for quotations are identified in the text by the abbreviations below. The editions used are those given in the bibliography. Where possible I have chosen the Penguin edition.

AS	*The Aunt's Story*
ES	*The Eye of the Storm*
FG	*Flaws in the Glass*
FL	*A Fringe of Leaves*
LD	*The Living and the Dead*
Letters	*Letters*, ed. David Marr
Life	David Marr, *Patrick White: A Life*
RC	*Riders in the Chariot*
SM	*The Solid Mandala*
Speaks	*Patrick White Speaks*
TA	*The Twyborn Affair*
TM	*The Tree of Man*
V	*The Vivisector*
Voss	*Voss*

CHRONOLOGY

1912   Born 28 May in flat in Knightsbridge, London. Brought back to Australia at the age of six months.

1916   Father (Dick) buys Lulworth, a large house in Kings Cross, Sydney, where much of White's childhood is spent.

1925   Sent to public school, Cheltenham College, England.

1929   Returns to Australia and works as jackeroo. Writes first novel, 'The Immigrants', and begins second novel, 'Sullen Moon', both unpublished.

1931   Back in Sydney, prepares for Cambridge exams and writes third unpublished novel, 'Finding Heaven'.

1932   Studies modern languages at Cambridge. Spends time in Germany to improve his German.

1935   Book of poems, *The Ploughman*, published by P. R. Stephensen, backed financially by White's parents. Some poems published in the *London Mercury*, and one republished in *The Best Poems of 1935*. Plays 'Bread and Butter Women' and 'The School for Friends' presented at Sydney's Bryants' Playhouse, promoted by his mother.

1936   Lives in London and has an affair with Roy de Maistre, who introduces him to modernism. Under de Maistre's influence, begins to rework his novel 'The Immigrants' as *Happy Valley*.

1937   Short story, 'The Twitching Colonel', published in *London Mercury*.

1938   Father dies. White has skit in successful London revue *Nine Sharp*.

1939   *Happy Valley* published in Britain and praised by British critics. Goes to US. Continues to write 'Nightside', a novel never published, about an Australian dancer who lives a second life in Paris and is murdered by a psychotic. Begins *The Living and the Dead*.

1940   *Happy Valley* published by Ben Huebsch at Viking in US. Returns to New York at beginning of war, and continues to write *The Living and the Dead* there. It is accepted by Viking but turned down by a number of British publishers.

1941   *The Living and the Dead* published by Viking in US, and Routledge in UK. Joins Royal Air Force and is sent to North Africa as an intelligence officer. Meets Manoly Lascaris in Alexandria. *Happy Valley* wins Australian Literature Society's Gold Medal.

1943   In North Africa begins planning a novel about a megalomaniacal Australian explorer. Writes an adaptation of Henry James's *The Aspern Papers* for the theatre.

1946   After being demobilised, returns to London. Begins *The Aunt's Story*, which is partly a rewriting of 'Sullen Moon'. Leaves for Australia in October.

1947   *The Aunt's Story* published in US and UK. Decides to stay in Sydney and begins work on what will become *Voss*. His play 'Return to Abyssinia' produced in a small theatre in London. Writes the play *The Ham Funeral*.

1948   Buys Dogwoods, a small farm at Castle Hill. Is discouraged by reception of *The Aunt's Story* and almost stops writing.

1950   Begins to write what will become *The Tree of Man*.

1954   Manuscript of *The Tree of Man* greeted with enthusiasm by Huebsch at Viking, but rejected by British publishers.

1955   *The Tree of Man* published in US, to enthusiastic reviews.

1956   *The Tree of Man* published in UK by Eyre & Spottiswoode, to good British reviews, and becomes an Australian bestseller, despite A. D. Hope's ambivalent review in the *Sydney Morning Herald*.

1957   *Voss* published in US and UK.

1958   Wins Miles Franklin Award. Publishes the essay 'The Prodigal Son' in *Australian Letters*. *The Aunt's Story* republished in Britain with a Nolan cover. Begins *Riders in the Chariot*.

1961   *Riders in the Chariot* appears. Wins Miles Franklin Award
        again. Governors of the Adelaide Festival reject *The Ham
        Funeral*, causing worldwide controversy. In anger, White
        writes *The Season at Sarsaparilla*. Begins *A Fringe of Leaves*,
        which over the next few years he thinks of first as a film,
        then as an opera.

1962   Writes a series of short stories, later published as *The Burnt
        Ones*. 'Down at the Dump' published by *Meanjin*. *The
        Season at Sarsaparilla* produced successfully in Adelaide and
        Melbourne. Writes short story 'A Cheery Soul' (published in
        London Magazine), which will become his third play.

1963   *The Season at Sarsaparilla* produced in Sydney, to abuse
        from the tabloids. In Melbourne, *A Cheery Soul* very badly
        reviewed and a box-office failure. In Adelaide, *Night on Bald
        Mountain* does reasonably well at the box office but not
        with the critics. Mother dies. Inherits half his father's estate,
        and puts Dogwoods up for sale.

1964   *The Burnt Ones* (a collection of his short stories) published.
        Buys a house in Centennial Park, Sydney. Begins *The Solid
        Mandala*.

1965   A collection of *Four Plays* published in London.

1966   *The Solid Mandala* published, first in New York then
        London. Writes short stories 'A Woman's Hand' and 'The
        Full Belly'. Begins a novel called 'The Binoculars and Helen
        Nell', which he never completes.

1967   Begins *The Vivisector*. Writes short story 'Five Twenty'.

1969   Appears in anti-Vietnam-war demonstration in defiance of
        the Crimes Act.

1970   *The Vivisector* published by Jonathan Cape, his new British
        publisher. Begins writing *The Eye of the Storm*. Appears for
        the defence in a trial against *Portnoy's Complaint*.

1972   Protests against plans to demolish Centennial Park houses
        (including his own) to make way for sports ground.

1973   Awarded Nobel Prize and made Australian of the Year.
        The Eye of the Storm published in doubled print run because
        of Nobel Prize. Returns to *A Fringe of Leaves*.

1974   *The Cockatoos*, a collection of short stories, published.

	Becomes involved in campaign to save Fraser Island. First Patrick White Prize awarded to Christina Stead.
1976	*A Fringe of Leaves* published.
1978	*The Night the Prowler* opens Sydney Film Festival, but is a critical and box-office failure.
1979	*The Twyborn Affair* appears in November, and is a best-seller in Australia.
1981	His autobiography, *Flaws in the Glass*, is published.
1986	*Memoirs of Many in One* appears.
1987	*Five Uneasy Pieces* published.
1990	Patrick White dies, 30 September.

1　THE CAREER

Patrick White became a writer just about as soon as he could: he was first published, in the children's pages of a newspaper, when he was nine. At primary school he circulated serials around class, and continued to scribble away through his school days. This urge to write — what were its sources? The question is impossible to answer satisfactorily but it is worth invoking at the beginning of a brief study of his life and work because it does take us some way into what he wrote years later as a professional novelist. We can say that White became a writer at least partly because he was encouraged to be one by his snobbish, doting and intimidating mother, a mother who expressly wanted her son to be a genius. This particular mode of motherly love had an immense impact on the writer that White turned out to be. It installed what we can call (with minimal Freudian overtones) a double, Oedipal relation at the heart of his texts. It is easy to read many of his works as enacting the desire to rid himself of the maternal origins of his will to write by destroying his mother in his writing. But they are also strategies to perpetuate his mother's desire, even sometimes by becoming her through his writing. That his will to write did not simply belong to him matters most, I think, because it meant that his identity as a writer (which increasingly meant his identity as a person *tout court*) was never quite his own. His identity was fragile and dispersed so that he could not answer the question 'Who *is* Patrick White?' except by saying that he was many people, most of them, as it turned out, fictional — his characters — and many of them women. And the exteriority of his will to write helps explain how difficult it was for him to write at all: it was a curse, a constant effort and something that, at the level of style and sentence-formation, he did not do very well, as critics and publishers often pointed out.

Glamourised by maternal love and ambition, his writing was an element in his larger will to present himself in front of a public, to make a spectacle of himself. As a schoolboy he was stage-struck and wanted to be not just an actor but a star — an ambition in which he fantasised that his sister, Suzanne, might join him. There exists a marvellous early family photograph in which young Patrick, about ten years old, poses madly while his mother stares proudly at him, ignoring everybody else, while his embarrassed father looks down at the ground. It is a picture of a tense, incommunicative family in which White could think of himself as the 'cuckoo' that his conventional parents had hatched (*FG* 10). What is also pictured is the love of posing that led him in later life to complain (echoing Philip Larkin): 'I don't want to go around pretending to be myself' (*Letters* 527), as well as to claim the opposite in his Nobel Prize acceptance speech: 'My flawed self has only ever felt intensely alive in the fictions I create' (*Speaks* 42).

If writing provided White with a kind of theatre, a stage on which he could create and enact parts of his fragmented self for others, it also drew from a very different, in some ways more powerful, mode of creating illusions. White begins his autobiography, *Flaws in the Glass*, by telling a story about how as a boy he set out to kill a teacher by making a wax model and sticking pins into it. His creativity here is a tool in the service of an aggressive anti-authoritarianism. His capacity for hatred was to become legendary, and there is a sense in which his novels remain carefully constructed magic curses directed against those who he thought thwarted his freedom and vision. And his belief in magic, or at least his willingness to see if magic worked, went further: for him, especially in his novels, the world might possess patterns and relations of which rationality has no notion. Voss's mystical communication with his fiancée Laura across the Australian desert is the best-known magical moment of this kind in his novels. In fact White's invocation of hidden correspondences and, in particular, his capacity to regard objects in the world as fragments of eternity, enabled him to relate to the world in a mode that was simultaneously spiritual and textual — as it had been for the symbolist writers ever since, say, the French poet Charles Baudelaire. It enabled him to organise his novels as if they imitated a structure in the world, but not the social, secular world. That is, the structure of his novels repeatedly relies on affinities or epiphanies that (supposedly) articulate a religious rather than a secular order.

These two aspects of White's writing, the theatrical and the spiritual, do not cohere. What could be more worldly, more secular, than the theatre, with its implication that what we are is the roles that we play? But who could be less actorly than, say, White's character Arthur Brown, in relation to his marbles, those solid mandalas, in the novel of that name? Because the theatrical and the spiritual do not cohere, they create highly charged eddies of (usually sexualised) ambivalence. Nothing seems less performative than Voss's abasement as he washes the shit from his companion Le Mesurier's dying body in *Voss*—unless it is precisely a performance to and for himself and the God he ostensibly does not believe in. White spins out his texts driven by the epistemological and moral energy generated by the friction between these two orders, the spiritual and the theatrical, represented later in his career by the artist Hurtle Duffield of *The Vivisector* on the one side and the actor Sir Basil Hunter in *The Eye of the Storm* on the other. In general his novels represent action as essentially theatrical and this often hollows out his characters' spiritual claims, except, as we shall see, when they are utterly passive, about to die. Near death and closure, characters' acts often produce textual patterns designed to point towards spiritual order in the world. Out of this tension, writing novels became a way in which White could all at once affirm and deny both his own spirituality and his own theatricality by playing one off against the other. He did so finally in the interests of an aggressive drive that was, in first place, directed towards himself (not least towards his sexuality, which he never wholly accepted), then towards his family and, finally, though not simply by extension, towards the wider society around him.

Literary institutions

Some of these ideas will be developed further in chapters to come, but it is important not to write as if White's career can be analysed simply in terms of private drives and struggles. That is too simple. Patrick

White was acclaimed as Australia's greatest novelist partly for reasons that bore little direct relation to what he actually wrote.

At one level he became 'Patrick White', the great writer, inside a set of literary institutions — publishing houses, university English departments, media review pages, literary agencies, copyright laws, literary prizes and so on. At another level, he became a great writer in relation to larger, constantly shifting social formations: to his class, to his generation, to his sexuality and so on. At still another level, it was his luck and fate to write just when Australia needed a great writer and there was a transnational cultural infrastructure through which it could produce one for world consumption.

In White's case, literary institutions had an international reach partly because he came from a family (more than a class) that did not think of itself as simply Australian. As they — or rather as his mother — saw it, the family ought to live at the centre of the world, and that centre did not lie in the antipodes. More importantly, perhaps, White's crucial literary relationships were made with overseas individuals and institutions because writers could not gain international prestige by publishing in Australia. The local publishing industry was very small and dominated by Britain. As John Curtain notes:

> In 1948 when the Australian Book Publishers Association (ABPA) was founded, only about 15 per cent of the books sold in Australia were of local origin. In 1953, when 24 per cent of all British book exports went to Australia, only three Australian publishers, Angus and Robertson, Melbourne University Press and FW Cheshire produced more than ten titles during the year.[1]

The local industry was so weak because the Australian book trade was regulated by copyright and trade agreements with Britain, especially the Net Book Agreement, which had an Australian Statement of Terms that set out conditions of supply and pricing. The British connection was not confined to book production: despite the long tradition of literary nationalism, reviews in influential Australian papers such as the *Sydney Morning Herald* and the Melbourne *Age* still often consisted of reprints from the British weeklies, a practice that did not begin to die away until the late 1970s, and has not yet quite disappeared.

It was White's relation with his American publisher, Ben Huebsch, that secured his career. David Marr rightly calls Huebsch 'the rock on which Patrick White's career was built' (*Life* 198). In fact Huebsch was one of the most important figures in twentieth-century English literature. Huebsch had negotiated the switch by many big-name modernist writers from small presses, usually funded by patronage, to the large, market-oriented publishing houses. He had been responsible for the US publication of the two writers who were most important to White's literary formation — D. H. Lawrence and James Joyce — having brought *Dubliners* and *A Portrait of the Artist as a Young Man* to the American public as long ago as 1916. When he merged his firm with Viking Press in 1925, he prepared the way for modernist novelists to gain acceptance outside the restricted world of little magazines and the avant-garde. It is important to note that Huebsch's decision to publish White was a decision to support precisely the kind of writing upon which his reputation had rested, to reproduce the canon he had helped to make. It was perhaps no accident that, once Huebsch had retired and White became less dependent on him for support and prestige, White's writing moved away from the Lawrence–Joyce–Woolf mode — models that mark his work up until, say, *The Solid Mandala*.

White's lines of contact with Huebsch were as much social as professional. He knew Huebsch through a network that consisted partly of a transatlantic gay connection and partly of a group of internationalised fans of modernism. This network seems to have been much more important to the dissemination of his work than his literary agent in England, Juliet O'Hea of the Curtis Brown agency. White first met Huebsch through the modernist poet Jean Starr Untermeyer, to whom he was introduced by George Plank (a gay designer and art-director famous for his *Vogue* covers), to whom in turn he was introduced by José Mamblas (White's lover of the time, a snobbish upper-class Spanish diplomat), whom he met indirectly through the British-based Australian modernist painter Roy de Maistre, who had also been White's lover, and of whom White wrote 'Roy de Maistre introduced me to abstract painting about 1936. Before that I had only approached writing as an exercise in naturalism' (*Letters* 170). De Maistre, indeed, was largely responsible for converting White to modernist culture as a whole. So White's career was made in the interactions between his mother's cultural geography, his own social and sexual relations, and the larger literary industry he needed to work in.

White's reputation was originally built in America, and was then transferred, more or less simultaneously, to Australia and the UK. This may seem odd, but this circuit of cultural capital was characteristic of the postwar shift in which the US replaced Britain as Australia's foremost ally. The American literary world was also much more hospitable to modernism than its British counterpart. In Britain after the war, neither reviewers nor publishers welcomed difficult, highly individuated (if still derivative) art writing of White's kind. Among White's early works, only his first published novel, the pre-war *Happy Valley*, was reasonably well reviewed by British critics as a whole, and the reason for that is obvious enough: the novel represents life in a small New South Wales rural town as almost unbearably narrow, thereby confirming metropolitan prejudices. At this point of his life, White, like his mother, mimicked British disdain of colonial life.

In part, this difference between British and US literary cultures was a consequence of the US publishing industry's sheer size: publishers could afford experiments, and did not have to receive good reviews in a small number of weeklies for their novels to be successful. But the British also moved away from the modernism associated with Joyce and Lawrence because novelists — not to mention reviewers and publishers — were preoccupied with interrogating and upholding various versions of Britishness at a time when Britain's cultural hegemony over the Anglophone world was lapsing. By and large, White's British male contemporaries — Graham Greene, Kingsley Amis and Angus Wilson, for example — were less experimental than White himself, and far less so than American writers such as Paul Bowles, William Gaddis, Jack Kerouac and William Burroughs, all of whom make White seem old-fashioned, a throwback to pre-war modernist models. Lawrence Durrell, whose *Alexandria Quartet* gained a huge reputation during the period of White's rise to fame, was a British exception; but Durrell's narrative 'experimentalism', such as it was, remained in the service of what White called a 'meretricious brilliance', a striving after exoticism (*Letters* 167). On the other hand, the realist British novelists wished to retrieve and reproduce social actuality as if to hold it in place against an outside world that they could not dominate. Unlike White, they were not able to repeat the older modernist spiritual and transgressive experiments; unlike the Americans, they did not live in, and could not creatively respond to, an affluent society flooded with consumer durables and well-paid middle-class jobs (for men).

The difference between the two major national Anglophone literary cultures in the postwar period is nowhere clearer than in the American and British publishers' very different responses to *The Tree of Man*, the novel that did more than any other to establish White's reputation. After reading the manuscript in 1956, Huebsch telegrammed 'VIKING CONGRATULATES YOU ON BEAUTIFUL PROFOUNDLY IMPRESSIVE FULFILMENT OF EXPECTATIONS', while his British publisher, Routledge, wondered what it was supposed to be about (*Life* 298). Even so, by the time *Riders in the Chariot* appeared in 1961, White was seen as a coterie writer in the US — mainly, I would argue, because there his writing style and project appeared increasingly obsolete by comparison with his adventurous American art-novelist contemporaries, yet did not appeal to the middlebrow market for serious novels, which was dominated at the time by writers such as John Updike and Saul Bellow. This meant that, in particular, White never enjoyed good reviews in *Time* magazine, an important arbiter of middlebrow literary taste.

As the 1950s went on, it became increasingly difficult for the media to deal with White, who could be called a late modernist writer in the tradition of Joyce and Lawrence, but lacked their newness, intensity and scandalousness. So, for instance, White failed in his efforts to get his stories published in American magazines. He sent 'Being Kind to Titina' to *Harper's Magazine*, which cut and rewrote it in house style. White withdrew the story and never tried to publish work in such magazines again. During the same period he became increasingly accepted in Britain, because the British came to see this 'colonial writer' as one of their own. The pattern of his reception and rejection in these literary institutions influenced the kind of cultural figure that White came to be.

What about his reception in Australia? It did not begin well. *Happy Valley* was attacked in Australia for condescension and failure to affirm the local culture. Even so, in 1941 it won the Australian Literature Society's Gold Medal. White's second published novel, *The Living and the Dead*, which is set in London and has no Australian references at all, appeared during the war and was therefore neglected, though it received a pretty negative review from Douglas Stewart in the *Bulletin*. But the most famous Australian attack on White was A. D. Hope's 1956 review of *The Tree of Man* in the *Sydney Morning Herald*. Hope's review contained a sentence that was to become famous: 'When so few Australian novelists can write prose at all, it is a great pity to see Mr. White, who shows on every page some touch of the born writer, deliberately choose as his medium this pretentious and illiterate verbal sludge' (*Life* 310). White's next novel, *Voss*, was received no better by Australian critics than by the British, who again noted the 'curdling' of the prose.

There was, however, an element of exaggeration in White's later complaints about the Australian critics' hostility.[2] At this stage of his career, White's appeal was declining faster in the US than in Britain and Australia: *Voss* sold 9000 copies in the US, against *The Tree of Man*'s 16,000. The next novel, *Riders in the Chariot* (1961), sold 8000 copies in the US, as against 9500 copies in Australia and 9000 in Britain (*Life* 382). *The Vivisector* only sold 4000 copies in the US, but more than twice that number in both Australia and Britain. The Australian reviews for that novel were excellent, and thereafter he was securely canonised as Australia's greatest novelist (all the more so after the Nobel Prize in 1973); reviews of his later novels were generally respectful, if not always warm. And his last two full-length novels, *A Fringe of Leaves* and *The Twyborn Affair*, each of which in its own way moved out of high modernism, sold well by White's standards.

White's plays won no such critical respect (and only occasionally received enthusiastic audience responses) and White's 1979 foray into films with *The Night the Prowler* was such a failure that it prevented him from achieving his ambition of scripting other films. Indeed, even as a novelist, it seems White was more praised and bought than actually read. A University of Melbourne survey of Australian readers of serious literature in 1993 and 1994 revealed a comparative lack of interest in White, and in the early 1960s a librarian was quoted in the press as saying 'No-one will read them [White's novels]. Each comes out in a blaze of publicity. In the case of *Voss* the library purchased twenty two copies. We got rid of some of them for 5/– a copy, and the last was reduced to 2/– a copy' (*Life* 391).

Yet, when it came to his canonisation, the fact that White was not especially read or readable was as much a help as a hindrance. For most of the past century, a writer has had to require readerly effort to achieve canonisation, at least in the academy. This was one of the fundamental features of modernist culture, for which art stood apart from easily consumed products of the larger-scale cultural industries.

Canonisation

White's canonisation was a complex process, involving literary institutions from several different countries. White's reputation, for example, owes much to the successful development of a 'modern classics' genre in the art-paperback market from the late 1950s. Perhaps nothing was more important to White's canonisation than the publication of *Voss* as a Penguin modern classic in 1960 (which was followed by the appearance of *The Aunt's Story* as a Penguin). Yet canonisation could not simply happen in the mainstream publishing houses and media reviews. In the modern literary world, the canonisation of contemporary writers happens most decisively when reputations that have been established in the weekly media are transferred into the monthly or quarterly literary magazines, and generally from there into the academic journals, which publish more narrowly scholarly and critical writing.

It also happens when writers begin to win important literary prizes — which are designed to produce contemporary canons as well as sales. As far as literary prizes go, White was to go on to win the big one, the Nobel, but by that time he was already established as a modern classic. More important perhaps to the literary world (as against the world at large) was his winning the first W. H. Smith & Son Literary Award for *Voss* in Britain in 1959, a win that owed less to the publication of *Voss* itself in 1957 than to the fact that *Voss* followed the 1955 American success of *The Tree of Man* so closely and that in 1958 *The Aunt's Story*, which had been almost totally overlooked when it first appeared, was republished in hard cover to a chorus of critical praise.

By the time writing about White moved from the review pages of the dailies and weeklies to the 'serious' literary and academic journals, a certain discourse about White was already in place. This was a discourse that emphasised White's 'depth' and the search for 'unity' that was thought to mark his fictions. To take one example, the British critic Edwin Muir, in his early and favourable review of *The Living and the Dead*, remarked:

> He examines, or rather enters into, the world of experience, ordinary and extraordinary, with an insistence which itself is a gift; for the essential mark of the writer who illuminates life for us is that he does not stop where other writers stop, content to reach an approximate stage, but pursues his search for meaning . . . the close investigation of thought and feeling is never pursued for its own sake; in all the parts there is a sense of the whole. (*Life* 209)

This was the rhetoric taken up by R. F. Brissenden in an article published in *Meanjin* in 1959 — the first essay written about White from a university department of English:

> we are meant to feel that all his central characters move toward the revelation and realisation of some truth . . . and that it is only when they have been able to grasp and understand it with all its implications that the pattern of their lives becomes meaningful to them, and to the reader.[3]

It should go almost without saying that this kind of Utopian and celebratory critical rhetoric does not accurately reflect White's aggressive, sexualised fictions.

Although White's reputation was made overseas, he first became the object of academic attention in Australia. An apparent irony nestles here: White was famously dismissive of academics, particularly Australian academics. When Huebsch asked him how *Voss* would do in Australia, he replied 'there will be the usual outcry from those who expect a novel to be a string of pedestrian facts, and from the critics, themselves mostly writers, or worse still, "professors"' (*Life* 320). And there are hints in his correspondence and public statements that he actually produced the kind of novels he did against his idea of the Australian critics.

This struggle between the creative writer and the academic critic is commonplace, indeed constitutive, because the writer is dependent on the critics for his or her place in the canon, but the critics anoint writers on their own terms, in discourses that claim mastery over the writing itself. Indeed, critics gain prestige to the extent that they can exceed a writer's own self-interpretation. This is why tensions between critics and writers are structural or constitutive rather than contingent.

Still, White's own appeal to the academy needs to be accounted for. One reason was that the values he expressed in his fictions were in harmony with a range of realignments in contemporary Australian culture. In the late 1950s and throughout the 1960s, traditional versions of cultural nationalism, nostalgic for the great days of the 1890s, for mateship, for rural Australia, began to be displaced. On the surface, it may appear strange that White's reputation was made in novels that were profoundly critical, not only of the 'Australian legend' that Russel Ward was reinventing at the time, but also of contemporary Australian ways of life, such as suburbia, middle-class affluence and love of sport. But White could become the great Australian writer as an anti-Australian (and, if it comes to that, as a closeted homosexual), because he connected to the national culture at what we can call its colonial/postcolonial switching point: the moment when the nation was beginning to stop conceiving of itself as a colony and instead was beginning to consider itself an independent nation-state among other nation-states.

At this moment, it became increasingly important for Australia to acquire cultural canons: to increase its cultural capital in competition with other national cultural heritages. At this moment it also became possible for the cultural canon to have a critical, reformist or spiritual intent, to work to other ends than those of — to take an instance almost at random — the 1956 literary anthology called *Australian Signposts* (successor to the best-selling *Australia Writes*), which aimed to 'show what a fascinating country Australia is' and to 'depict the honour and toughness, the sensitivity and courage of Australians at work and at home, in the country and in the city, on land and on sea, in peace and in war'.[4]

Nobody could accuse White of that kind of uncomplicated cultural nationalism. Indeed, a turn from such nationalisms was what was required if old colonialist images of Australianness were to be set aside, just as it was required if Australia were to avoid becoming as dependent on the US as it had once been on Britain. White's canonisation, then, is not just to be thought of simply in terms of literary prizes or of the academisation of the literary rhetoric that celebrated him, or of his passing appeal to an American taste for old-fashioned modernism, but in terms of Australia's refashioning of itself in a world order where British links could no longer actively be mobilised, and where the nation required uniquely national icons.

White's canonisation is part of a larger cultural shift, which saw the development of many kinds of institutions and critiques aimed at making Australia culturally richer and more autonomous. Let me name just a few: the setting up of the Elizabethan Theatre Trust to develop local drama in 1954; the Murray Report's recommendation to build new universities in 1957; the inauguration of the Adelaide Festival in 1960, and of the Australian Ballet in 1962; the construction of the Sydney Opera House from 1963 onwards; Donald Horne's 1964 book *The Lucky Country*, which turns the tables on White's anti-suburban aesthetic by conceding that the suburbs are not some failure of authentic Aussie life; the birth of a national daily newspaper, *The Australian*, the same year; the setting up of the Australian Conservation Foundation and Menzies' giving the green light to the establishment of a National Gallery in Canberra, both in 1965. The solidifying of White's reputation is an event in this series.

The switch from colonialist to postcolonialist cultural life did not occur without flashpoints. Indeed White's career itself provided some of the most notorious such sparks — such as the rejection of *The Ham Funeral* by the Governors of the Adelaide Festival in 1961 (the second year of the Festival's existence) on the grounds that 'Its complexity will limit its appeal to a few high intellectuals and even they would find it difficult to interpret the so called psychological aspects of the play' (*Letters* 186). This rejection made headlines the world over, and

White was presented in the role of great artist against provincial Philistines with an outmoded taste for social realism. That White provided Australia with its own version of the artist–Philistine clash, and one with international newsworthiness, only consolidated his canonisation.

I have been dealing with White as a novelist, and his novels will be almost the sole interest of this book, but White's work in the theatre is important to the configurations of his ultimate Australian success. For it was around the theatre that signs of the new non-colonialist Australian culture appeared most graphically, signs that, as White put it in a letter to Huebsch in February 1962, 'the change is taking place, only very, very slowly' (*Letters* 204). The 'change' that White mentions here was in fact double: on the one hand, it referred to Australia's moves towards cultural independence, on the other to the set of shifts and innovations that we now often associate with 'the Sixties'. If White became famous during the 1950s, his reputation could be extended into the next decades, and his work could maintain its relevance, because it was, however remotely, in dialogue with this double change.

White's interest in this dialogue is clearest in regard to his work in the theatre in the early 1960s. Again there are structural reasons for this. In its relation to a public and hence to the media, the theatre is more immediate than writing. It is also a collaborative art. For both these reasons, shifts of direction and cultural realignments can form and become apparent in theatre much more quickly than in the novel, for example. Certainly in 1961 White was convinced that a new cultural Australia was about to appear. After the Adelaide Festival had rejected *The Ham Funeral,* a student production was successfully mounted. To his delight he found that he 'spoke the same language' as the students who were interested in his theatrical work at a time when the establishment was dismissing it (*Letters* 192). Once again White's gayness was crucial; John Tasker, the young director to whom White entrusted his play, seduced White, at least figuratively.

As it turned out, White was buoyed by a great deal of Sixties postcolonialist cultural politics, of which the Adelaide controversy was an early indication. For the first time in his life he entered politics without reservation on the anti-imperialist side over Vietnam, and later became an important spokesperson for the anti-nuclear and environmental movements. Still his own values and work were never fully attuned to the Sixties. He rejected gay liberation (he only came out in the late 1970s), and he was even more contemptuous of the women's movement. Certainly the new Australian theatre later went in a direction very different from his own.

Yet White had written against the colonialist cringe and its obverse, traditional cultural nationalism, and had heroicised Australia's outsiders (to use a fashionable word of the time). Unlike Anglophile writers such as Martin Boyd or Hal Porter, he could maintain some kind of relevance in the first (transnational) postcolonial moment — that of the Sixties culture. To offer just one more example: his character Hurtle Duffield in *The Vivisector* seems to have much more powerful affinities with the ambience of a Brett Whitely, the *enfant terrible* of the Sixties, than with older Australian nationalist/modernist painters such as Arthur Boyd or Sidney Nolan. Whether these affinities will secure his reputation into the twenty-first century seems less certain. But the texts and cultural forces that have so far secured that reputation will concern us in what follows.

2　THE AUSTRALIAN

In this chapter I want to extend my argument that White's life and work need to be evaluated as part of a transitional moment in the emergence of postcolonial Australia. I am as interested in White's life as in his work, not just because one shapes the other, but because his life, like his work, was shaped by the postcolonial turn. To make my case, it will sometimes be necessary to move beyond White's career, and to outline Australia's slow retreat from colonialism.

Intellectual Australia

We know that the young Patrick White subscribed to international modernism. His early novels, *Happy Valley* and *The Living and the Dead*, broke from the Australian tradition as it was conceived by those critics who, beginning with the Australian Literature Society in 1899, had slowly turned 'Australian literature' into a canon. What did this tradition look like? At its heart lay the 1890s nationalists (especially Henry Lawson and Joseph Furphy) and later works in the realist mode intended to extend their values. To put the case simply, the struggle for a specifically Australian literary heritage was linked with that for a more egalitarian nation, and here Lawson and Furphy could be appealed to because they wrote, so it was thought, for the 'common man'. Later intellectuals committed to cultural nationalism — Vance and Nettie Palmer being perhaps the most important — championed realism as a literary mode because only realism seemed to have the potential to communicate to the nation as a whole. Intermittent forays into modernism in Australia were marginalised because they did not help build the nation in these terms.

At this point we need to sharpen the argument that White's canonisation marks a switch from colonialist to postcolonial cultural politics. To map the Australian intellectual scene in which he wrote, more subtle distinctions are required — all the more so because, after about 1957, various intellectual positions confronted each other around his work. Let us call the position occupied by the Palmers, as well as by writers such as Katharine Susannah Prichard, 'late-colonial realism'. Vance Palmer was especially important to this movement because, in line with most critics before the mid-1950s, he considered that Australian culture was not yet fully formed: it had to be constructed from the traces of the rural, egalitarian tradition that he had described in *The Legend of the Nineties* (1954). But the late-colonial realists also believed that Australia required its own culture, not just because it was a 'new' country from the colonisers' perspective, but because it was now being threatened by urbanisation and American-based popular culture. Palmer commented as early as 1921 that

Melbourne and Sydney stand for Australia nowadays. They provide . . . the artistic and literary ideals, the utopian and the national characteristics; and because they have no roots it is natural that all their products should have a second-hand flavour . . . picture theatres, gramophones, motor cars and villas are universal, and with them you can build a modern suburb in a week, one that, like the mule, is without pride of ancestry or hope of posterity.[1]

It seemed the era of pioneer colonialism could provide an image for cultural regeneration against such commodification and rootlessness.

How to consider White's mid-1950s novels in this context? White hated the suburbs too; like the realists, he rejected the urban establishment and contested the Americanisation of the life-world; in his own way, he also glorified the 'common man'. In *The Tree of Man* he even seemed to appeal to the settler-colonialist ethos. But he did so from somewhere new. As a result, the late-colonial realists were critical of his work. Prichard, for instance, gave *Voss* a negative review in *Overland* on the grounds that the novel appealed to 'sophisticated readers' and failed sufficiently to affirm the lives of its simple characters; implicitly, the novel was too pessimistic to encourage national cultural formation.[2] If White's work after *The Tree of Man* was by no means a radical break from late-colonial realism in its cultural politics, it disengaged from that tradition at the very least because it required readerly skills unavailable to 'ordinary Australians' as the realist tradition had figured them. It appealed to an unlocatable audience, identified neither as suburban nor as rural, neither as conventionally middle-class nor as working-class. In White the dream of a unified national culture based on some mode of ordinary Australianness had disappeared.

By the mid-1950s, cultural resuscitation was not to be found in evocations of the hard early days of settlement, nor in any other kind of ruralism. This was not because of any rethinking of the political morality of settlement itself; rather, the colonial realist program became impossible because urban lifestyles based on mass-produced consumer durables had become a 'second nature'. Their absence was now unimaginable. Urbanisation was a fact of Australian life: by 1966 14 per cent of Australians lived in rural settlements, as compared to 31 per cent in 1933, and by the 1950s managing suburbanisation was a central task of government, industry and the media.[3]

As colonialist nostalgia retreated under suburbanisation and the Americanisation of the so-called 'free world', a movement that I will call late-colonial transcendentalism took its place in Australian literary culture, with White as one of its standard-bearers, at least until *The Solid Mandala*. And it was White's transcendentalism, as well his modernist writing techniques, that marked him from his realist predecessors.

It is not as though late-colonial transcendentalism was simply part of a larger push towards postcolonialism. Transcendentalism also contested the postcolonial shift. This becomes apparent when we recall the form that Australian postcolonialism was to take. It turns around five main axes, some of which are already familiar. First, for a fully fledged postcolonialism, white settlement is not to be considered as the simple transplantation of European civilisation so much as a series of brutal expropriations from, and massacres of, local peoples, the history of which must be told from both sides. Second, Australian postcolonialism accepts the suburban nature of modern Australian life. Third, the ideal of national cultural unity, based on an image of the rural ordinary bloke, is replaced by the sense that Australia possesses irreducible ethnic differences (an orientation that was to contribute to official multiculturalism). Fourth, the living traditions of indigenous peoples are seen as crucial to the national cultural mix. And finally,

Australia is no longer considered as a far-flung province of Europe, but is placed at the edge of Asia. These axes of the postcolonial shift provide a frame through which we can read White's writing and career.

Instead of grasping the full implications of postcolonialism, transcendentalists like the young White replaced appeals to the colonialist past with appeals to various universal themes, which were often called 'metaphysical'. They attempted to detach contemporary Australian culture from its colonising past by claiming that Australian cultural identity was based on acknowledgement of 'the terror at the basis of being' as the critic Harry Heseltine put it in 1962, or 'the sense of spiritual darkness' in A. A. Phillips' phrase of 1958 — a thematic already established in Martin Boyd's *The Cardboard Crown* (1952).[4] According to these writers, Australian culture could still be Australian while pursuing 'universal' rather than 'local' *topoi*.

These notions were intensely debated during the 1950s and early 1960s. Today, from a postcolonial point of view, they are most usefully analysed as a recodifying of old ideas of Australian 'emptiness', which were signs both of nostalgia for Europe and of a disavowed white guilt over the invasion of the land. Invoking the universal tragedy of the human condition (a classic Eurocentric theme) was so seductive locally because it expressed the travails and horrors of white settlement while simultaneously concealing them.

The break with realism, then, happened not as a turn to explicit postcolonialism but as an internationalism whose tragic orientation predated modernism and whose most articulate recent instance was developed in pre-war France. What was to become a widespread 'apocalyptic' movement in Europe during the 1940s had emerged in an offshoot of French surrealism, led by Georges Bataille, who refused to follow André Breton into an alliance with communism, and who would attempt to replace modern categories such as the aesthetic or the political with a revivified sense of myth and sacrifice. This movement, at least with the work of Michel Leiris, pioneered the philosophical critique of Europeans' colonial past and present, but in Australia the new critics' transcendentalism was imported as a return to the timeless and spiritual, which was used to negotiate both Europe's crisis of faith in its own history and colonialism's loss of legitimacy.

In Australia, the transcendental move was also designed to enrich national culture. White often declared this quite forthrightly. Asked by an interviewer for the literary magazine *Southerly* 'Looking back over your novels, would you be conscious of certain preoccupations recurring, or of particular things you have tried to do?' he replied:

Life in Australia seems to be for many people pretty deadly dull. I have tried to convey a splendour, a transcendence, which is also there, above the human realities . . . I wanted to suggest my own faith in these superhuman realities.[5]

From this perspective, realism merely confirmed the status quo; it could not 'heighten life', as White put it. White's determination to fill the country's emptiness and ugliness, however, compelled it to share Europe's 'tragic' fate.

What spiritualising meant technically for White as a novelist was the insertion of 'symbols' into his writings. These symbols existed beneath the text's surface, in that they required active interpretation and uncovering. To find the text's hidden significance was also to find the country's purpose. As White wrote to his cousin, 'I felt the life [in Australia] was, on the surface, so dreary, ugly, monotonous, there must be something hidden in it to give it a purpose, and so I set out to find a secret core, and *The Tree of Man* emerged' (*Life*, 284).

In fact transcendentalism allowed literary intellectuals to move beyond colonialist ways of thinking while maintaining the colonial realists' attack on Australia's drift to suburbanism and consumerism. Transcendentalism joined Australian literature to Australian history and culture in terms grand enough to bypass everyday contexts, especially the political context that had been the Palmers' primary frame of reference. And it was because transcendentalist literature was by nature esoteric — it possessed a 'secret core' — that it was no longer an expression of ordinary Australianness; the texts, with their 'symbols' and mythical resonances, demanded a kind of close reading best taught in universities (where a 'new criticism' based on such reading practices was becoming standardised). White's scorn for professors needs to be understood in relation to his dependency on them in this specific situation.

Yet a novel like *The Tree of Man* could be praised by the new critics because it filtered transcendentalism through colonial realism (in the essay cited above, A. A. Phillips declared that 'Patrick White is more traditional than is generally supposed'). However opaque *The Tree of Man* was, it was also familiar — despite everything, it was directly related to Australian popular-cultural iconography. Stan and Amy can be seen as versions of Bob Freeland and his wife — two characters whose life-stories were narrated in a famous 1948 advertising campaign through which the banks fought nationalisation by Chifley's ALP. Bob, like Stan, lived in his own house, with a wife and two children, and had 'fair curly hair on his head and forearms'.[6] But Stan and Amy relate to the cosmos rather than to the messy politics of nation-building. Indeed the hard Australian politics of 1910–1950 is absent from White's *oeuvre*: that is one sign of his international transcendentalism.

Living early postcoloniality

I have been discussing the switching point between late colonialism and postcolonialism as it took the form of transcendentalism in literature. But, useful as these terms are in providing us with the pattern of historical transformation during White's early working life, neither his work nor his life wholly fits such abstract patterns. On the one hand, no schema can account for White's tangled, overdetermined relation to Australia. On the other, he did not live out his relation to Australia simply as an individual.

Let us take the crucial instances: his vocation as a novelist and his postwar decision to repatriate. We know that expatriate Australian art-writers, particularly those who came from rich families, had long regarded Australia as debased. For older expatriate writers such as Martin Boyd or Christina Stead, the problem was not so much that civil society in Australia was thin — lacking in occasions for casual sociability, say, compared with European urban street life — as that Australian culture did not provide a sustaining understanding of how to live. Yet even these writers, who had no truck with the nationalism of the stay-at-home realists, hovered between a sense of the country's lacks and a sense of its capacity to provide a new beginning. In the expatriate Australian novel this indecisiveness is most tellingly expressed by Henry Handel Richardson's *The Fortunes of Richard Mahony*, where Mahony's nomadic quest for a satisfactory cultural life leaves him stranded between Britain and Australia, between the country and the city, between consumerism and asceticism, unable finally to settle anywhere at all.

Patrick White lived and wrote out of this tension; he was something of a Richard Mahony himself. But, unlike Boyd or Stead, he lived most of his working life in Australia. His return was a conscious decision, a giving up of Europe as a place to live in. *The Aunt's Story*, although written before his decision to return, is especially revealing of the young White's attitude to living in Australia as against living in exile. It is a fiction about national homelessness, about being placed between national cultures rather than in a national culture. (It is important that Theodora's family's beloved Australian house — an old settler family's homestead — is named Meroë, the most southerly latitude in the old, pre-Columbus *mappa mundi* and, as a centre of African civilisation, never fully incorporated into the West.) Yet Theodora's attempt to expatriate herself finally ends in disaster, not because of any personal history but because Europe is going up in flames. White's presentation of the burning hotel in the *jardin exotique* section of the novel, in which he uses lessons learnt from the 'Circe' episode of *Ulysses* as well as from Djuna Barnes, functions as an allegorical emblem of a devastated and demoralised Europe.

The war compelled White (and many others) to rethink European history. Leaving aside the extraordinary impact of the first nuclear weapons (which remain an unnamed presence in White's work of the period), the Holocaust revealed once and for all that Europe's claim to be the world centre of civilised life-practices, a global cultural heritage and rational, just, universalisable values, was hollow. Europe's civil society and cultural heritage had not prevented genocide. Japan's early successes against the West, along with the colonial contribution to the war effort, also helped urge forward the colonies' will to independence. White had a direct experience of this: his sympathy for societies outside the great imperial nations derived from the war in North Africa, where he met his lifelong partner, Manoly Lascaris.

In a sense the Second World War provided Europe with a harder lesson than that imposed by the First World War, which had been widely experienced as a tragedy imposed by 'them' (the establishment) upon 'us' (the ordinary people), and had not succeeded in denting Eurocentrism. As White knew, having spent time as a student in pre-war Germany, Nazism belonged to the ordinary German people, in conspiracy with establishment forces throughout Europe.

The weakening of the European ideal contributed to the gradual emergence of the postcolonial, multicultural Australia in which White's reputation was secured. It also helps to explain his alliances, in both his life and his writing, with those who were then called 'New Australians' — those who shared his migration from Europe (strange as it may be to put it like that) — just as it helps us see how he was prepared to take the anti-imperialist side over Vietnam in 1966, although at the time he was a political conservative. And there is no doubt that his experience of the war, his sense of Europe's decline and his difficult return to his native country are threaded through his later work. Images of European conflagrations, apocalyptic visitations of chaos, appear again and again — from the burning hotel in *The Aunt's Story* to the graphic, autobiographical Blitz scenes in his last full-length novel, *The Twyborn Affair*. There are subtler instances too. Read against the war, *Voss* becomes a portrait of a Hitler figure, as popularly conceived, a leader with a will to power so disconnected from moral values and other people's lives that he can lead nowhere except to destruction.

In *The Aunt's Story* this ambivalent cultural condition — being at home neither in Australia nor elsewhere — is, characteristically, folded into a familial and sexual one. Theodora's rebellion against her parents, her inability to marry, her unfemininity (which is a gender-inverted mirror-image of White's self-ascribed femininity), are as important to her homelessness as her failure to connect wholeheartedly to Australia, America or Europe. This brings us to another, though connected, level of White's overdetermined relation to Australia: he related to it not just as a member of a pastoral family, a subject of history and so on, but as a homosexual, a modernist aesthete, and his mother's son. There can be no doubt that White's return to Australia was partly motivated by his desire not to live in the same place as Ruth White, his mother, who had moved to London after her husband's death, and the Oedipal nature of his repatriation helps make sense of the way that his response to the country was mediated through her image of Australia. It helps to explain why he returned to a country he often declared he hated, and why his writing attempted to build up a culture it so fiercely criticised.

It is as if White repudiated his mother's values only by incorporating them into himself: he rejected his mother's rejection of Australia, but he also internalised it. Like his mother's Australia, White's is vulgar, rigid, far from the centres of civility and doomed to produce bad imitations of overseas styles. For White it could always, despite everything, once again become what Laura Trevelyan in *Voss* called 'a remote colony', a place where only second-best lives could be lived (*Voss* 9).

A number of further points need to be made to account more carefully for White's personal relationship to Australia. To begin with, his experience of England was unsettling: despite his official Englishness, he was — or at least felt himself to be — positioned as a 'colonial', especially at school and university. This sense of rejection was more than a biographical accident: one path towards postcoloniality, if a minor one, is the way in which the old high colonialist dream of mirroring Europe, forming truly European settlements and subjects in the colonies, came adrift precisely because the settlers were irretrievably marked as colonial in the eyes of metropolitan culture. They remained 'mimic' people, however hard they tried. In *A Fringe of Leaves*, Ellen Roxburgh, who marries into the upper bourgeoisie, becomes a version of the young White in this regard: her strange accent has to be hidden from her new middle-class friends, and her discomfort in a stultified world in which she is an outsider is a displaced reminiscence of White's experience as an Australian in Britain. When Ellen first arrives in Van Diemen's Land, her sense of liberation, joined to a realisation that her new colonial life will bring with it new constrictions, is a version of the settler experience in returning to the colonies.

This brings us to the second point about Australia's difference from Europe as White conceived it. For Ellen, as for White, the Australian landscape possessed a vital, if mysterious, presence that was missing from the land's human population. This is how White invokes the landscape in his autobiography:

> It was landscape which made me long to return to Australia while at school in England. It was landscape more than anything which drew me back when Hitler's War was over. As a child at Mount Wilson and Rushcutters Bay, relationships with even cherished friends were inclined to come apart when I was faced with sharing surroundings associated with my own private mysteries, some corner where moss-upholstered steps swept down beside the monstera deliciosa, a rich mattress of slater-invested humus under the custard apples, or gullies crackling with smoky silence, rocks threatening to explode, pools so cold that the breath was cut off inside your ribs as you hung suspended like the corpse of a pale frog. (*Flaws* 16)

In this subtropical landscape, nature has regressed, become a partner for the pleasurable disorder of a child's body: it invites crouching, it keeps other people out. This is nature as Miss Hare in *Riders in the Chariot* inhabits it. Throughout White's work, the act of stooping down to touch the earth is extremely charged; only his most favoured characters do it.

Australian nature could be figured differently, though, as in this passage from *Flaws in the Glass*:

> I preferred a landscape. It answered my needs. More passive than the Monaro, it was also more sensual, sympathetic towards human flesh. Perhaps because a rare commodity, water played a leading part in my developing sexuality. I was always throwing off my clothes to bathe, either at the artesian bore during a pause from mustering, the water ejaculating warm and sulphurous out of the earth, or in the river flowing between the trunks of great flesh-coloured gums, to a screeching, flick-knife commentary by yellow-crested cockatoos, or at night in the hollow below the homestead if a good season had turned it into a lagoon. Here I was joined by the men who worked about the place . . . (*Flaws* 51)

Here the landscape, with its liquid ejaculations, is male but not phallic: it is as if nature invites you to have male sex only. And because it is nature itself that ejaculates, not a man, White avoids his residual homosexual guilt. It is likely that, at some level, White could fantasise his return to Australia as a return to a country where he could avoid and displace not just his mother, not just female sexuality, but the full implications of his own sexuality. Certainly it was a place where he escaped the homosexual networks that had been pivotal to his early career.

Australia as landscape, regressive and Oedipal as it may be, throws actual Australian society and its debasement into harsher relief. This is clearest in *Riders in the Chariot*, which marks the beginnings of White's attack on 'ordinary' Australia. Here the nation is materialistic, violent in its rejection of cultural difference, a hysterical place. The nation is embodied in the paranoias of its least tolerant citizens — particularly, given White's habitual misogyny, of ageing heterosexual women. Miss Hare's asexual nature worship stands against the murderous sexuality and suburban resentments of Mrs Jolley and Mrs Pask.

White himself recognised that he found it difficult to write about characters who were ordinarily Australian, because they quickly turned into superficial stereotypes. As he put it in a letter late in life:

> To return to this question of superficiality and density: it is the great prob-
> lem in writing about anything Australian; my (secret) solution is to ring in
> as many foreigners and eccentrics as possible and hope I can keep people
> interested through those. (*Letters* 360)

Yet even his distrust of Australian subjectivities and his hatred of sub-urban respectability could be metamorphosed into a political critique and applied, almost against itself, to more direct forms of nation-building. After the Whitlam dismissal, during negotiations for filming *Voss*, White attacked Kerr and Fraser as he had once attacked fictional characters like Mrs Jolley: 'When I wrote the novel [*Voss*] I was more involved with the journey than the preparations, but since recent weeks I'd like to see the "arrogant and philistine bourgeoisie" get a full broadside' (*Letters* 468).

Perhaps the strangest thing about White's move back to Australia is how, in certain scenes, he transposes European forms onto the local situation. In *Riders in the Chariot*, in particular, he imports into Sydney the xenophobias that had devastated Europe. As the novel ends, Mordecai Himmelfarb, that gentle Jewish refugee, is crucified by a mob of drunk Australian yobbos. This is not to say that Australia lacked (or lacks) ethnic hatreds. Indeed, while White was writing *Riders in the Chariot*, swastikas were being scrawled on Sydney walls, and in 1960 he attended protests against these unsettling outbreaks of anti-Semitism. Postwar European immigrants routinely met hostility and prejudice in a country that had considered itself a monoculture. Yet Himmelfarb's crucifixion in the suburban Sydney of the 1950s is wildly improbable. It is designed to demonstrate that, in its cruelty, Australia possesses possibilities of sacrificial transcendence — a belief that we can now see also expresses White's resistance to his mother, and the class, sexuality and gender that she embodies. Maybe it was because the possibility of recoding Australia spiritually was so privately overdetermined for White that he could pretend to himself that Sydney in the 1950s might repeat the horrors of Roman Jerusalem or Nazi Germany, and, in his Nobel Prize statement, ridicule critics who pointed out the implausibility of his vision.

The final point to be made about White's refusal of the expatriate option is that it belongs, if somewhat loosely, to a history of specifically colonial formations of the family. Especially during the colonial epoch, the Australian public sphere formed in and around pubs, gambling joints, brothels, a few theatres, newspapers. Social life in public spaces (and even, if less so, in print) was strongly masculine. Also Australians tended to be geographically mobile. All this meant that the nuclear family became more important than it was in metropolitan centres, despite White's fantasies of a male-sexualised setting. The heterosexual family was the social unit most easily transplanted into and across colonial settlements; it ensured the reproduction of the vulnerable white society. It ordered women's lives in particular.

Thus it is that Australia's two most successful expatriate art-novels — *The Fortunes of Richard Mahony* and Christina Stead's *The Man who Loved Children* — are both controlled and amazingly detailed screams of rage against fathers, written from the position of women trapped in father-dominated families. Both novels imagine the father's death, and in *The Fortunes of Richard Mahony* Richard's gradual physical and mental disintegration is lingered over with a glee and horror that cannot be disguised by the writing's apparent objectivity. If

Richardson takes revenge on the father by picturing him in death and decay, Stead presents her father as harming her by pre-empting not only her autonomy but her capacity to love. It is as if the father ensures that he is the only man a daughter can love, so that in making her love him he makes her hate him. In this way, for both novels, anger against the father becomes a perverse celebration of patriarchal energy and pride.

White reorders this strong form of Australian women exiles' writing for his homosexuality and his modernism. His target is his mother rather than his father. Many of his novels, from *The Living and the Dead* to *The Eye of the Storm*, turn around a mother's death, which seals his text's symbolism. It is a move that joins him to Joyce and Lawrence, who can only become the writers they are through public display of their aggression against their mothers as well as their grief and sense of responsibility for their mothers' deaths. Whereas his predecessors leave the family behind in their writing, White never does, because the family shapes his identification with the national culture. White's Australianness need not be thought about as simply in terms of the ways that he represents Australia. His connection to Australia is marked by the way in which he enacts a familial drama in his life and writings.

Colonial and indigenous Australia

How did White thematise Australia in his novels? As I have argued, his attempt to structure his texts through mythical themes — the will to dominate others and nature and its failure in *Voss*, the importance of the scapegoat to social cohesion and spirituality in *Riders in the Chariot*, the eternal values of the ascetic life in *The Tree of Man* — is a sign that White was a precursor to postcolonialism. A more direct indication of White's move out of colonialism, however, was that for him colonialism had to be historically re-created (it had to become learnt history rather than living memory, we might say) and that moments of early contact between the colonised and colonisers were particularly fascinating. For him after *The Tree of Man*, as for postcolonialists generally, it is as if a strong image of Australia might be found by looking back to the fateful moment when the two sides of the colonial divide first encountered each other — that is, when two autonomous cultures existed in the continent beyond any doubt.

In *Voss* and *A Fringe of Leaves*, the two novels he sets in the colonial era, White represents colonisation as a fragile settlement of a country that resists shaping by Europeans. In fact, the country even resists humanisation, and never becomes an easy place for habitation. It is a place where accidents and death seem to happen more often than elsewhere, but also a place where human (or European) will to power can be tested — and fail. As Laura of *Voss* says: 'Everyone is still afraid, or most of us, of this country, and will not say it. We are not yet possessed of understanding' (*Voss* 28). So, in relation to the coloniser, the land can become a sign of the radically inhuman, which can in turn be transformed into a sign of a transcendental tragic condition. This is especially so because, for White as for white settlers generally, Australia is an edge culture, not just far from Europe but on the edge of the 'country beyond', the great interior, available to test will and imagination (*FL* 154). As such, it is particularly revealing of authenticity because it strips away the merely social:

> a white light threatened to expose the more protected corners of human personality. Mr Roxburgh was fully exposed. In advancing towards this land's end, he felt the trapping of wealth and station, the pride in ethical and intellectual aspirations, stripped from him with a ruthlessness reserved for those who accept their importance or who have remained unaware of their pretentiousness. (*FL* 208)

Authentic contact with the inhuman reveals that individuals are not fully individuals at all: their individuality is a reflex of their financial and class position (their 'station') and then of their secular pride.

For White, no rigid border divides the community, in which individuals form personalities, from nature, which undoes those personalities. For him, Australian society never quite fosters organic, self-enclosed communities, which is both its problem and its power. To begin with, White was fascinated with the 'moral infection' (as he calls it in *A Fringe of Leaves*) resulting from Australia's origin as a penal colony (*FL* 82). So, to take just one instance, the unscrupulousness and energy that mark White's successful Australian men is first found in transportees such as Judd the emancipist in *Voss* and the philandering crook Garnet Roxburgh in *A Fringe of Leaves*. Ray in *The Tree of Man* shows the type in a late colonial setting. In one form or another, Australia will produce this kind of man over and over again: restless, driven to destroy others' happiness and security by forces he cannot understand. The male drive to move outside the family and to destroy communal trust expresses one way that the emptiness of the land and the horror of its history is lived out.

Being morally infected and empty, White's Australia is also fragmented. It contains families, of course, but also groups made up of individuals who share space almost by accident and do not draw anything of value from their contiguity: suburban neighbours in *The Tree of Man* or *The Solid Mandala*; more intensely and problematically, the explorers in *Voss*, or the characters who find themselves together in the Queensland wilderness in *A Fringe of Leaves*. Extreme situations (floods, desert, fires) only fuse these groups for a moment. Such communities without organisation, as we can call them, provide the stage for unmediated clashes of will, fits of desire and repulsion. To picture modern communities as bunches of individuals arbitrarily thrown together and threatened by crisis was already a literary commonplace (as in Conrad's *The Nigger of the 'Narcissus'*). In White, this became less a general condition of modernity than a specific condition of colonialism.

Sometimes individuals find affinities almost magically — the four central characters who share their vision in *Riders in the Chariot*, for example, or the disparate characters who become Hurtle Duffield's friends in *The Vivisector* — but it is only rejection by society that permits individuals who do share an authentic relation to the world to come together. White's logic is that being excluded from conventional norms draws people back to share the fundamentals of existence even as it makes them solitary.

Of all the limits to White's capacity to imagine a postcolonial Australia, the most important is his failure to absorb the consequences of settlement for indigenous peoples. *The Tree of Man*, which is an allegory of settlement, presents the land literally as *terra nullius*. Later, when it had become impossible to ignore prior Aboriginal presence, White failed adequately to conceive the dynamics of cultural contact from the Aboriginal side. It is relevant to note that, as late as the early 1960s, according to David Marr, he had never met an Aborigine (*Life* 360). This is not to say that he remained insensitive to the damage done to Aboriginal peoples by white settlement, though he seems never to have fully confronted the full meaning of the fact that his family fortune was based on the expropriation of the Kamilaroi people's country. His remains a postcolonialism of the colonisers rather than the colonised. For him, native peoples were victims but not agents: and a sure sign of this is that they were wholly available to be imagined by the great white writer.

There are moments when White considers colonial fragility in relation to the colonised peoples, even if in a displaced way. Here, for instance, Laura Trevelyan in *Voss* meditates on the Bonners' expensive Sydney house:

> It was now possible that the usually solid house, and all that it contained, that the whole civil history of those parts was presumptuous, and that the night, close and sultry as savage flesh, distant and dilating as stars, would prevail by natural law. (*Voss* 85)

'Night' — which in this text demands to be read as a sign of a universe without God or a knowable purpose — may swallow up colonial 'civil history'. In this passage colonial civil history's transcendental opposite, the Nietzschean universe without direction, manifests itself in that 'savage flesh'. At one level, it is in such a moment that White can admit that European settlement was based on illegitimate violence; yet, like Joseph Conrad in *Heart of Darkness*, he can do so only by cloaking this point in transcendental gestures and by figuring Aborigines through an old lexicon of primitivism in terms such as 'savagery', 'darkness' and 'night'.

Indeed, White's descriptions of rural Aborigines never wholly move past primitivism. *Voss*, the first novel to have important Aboriginal characters, is suffused with it. Take the moment when Brendan Boyle, a pastoralist living in the outback, introduces Voss to two Aborigines, Dugald and Jackie, who will accompany him in his expedition:

Alone, he and the blacks would have communicated with one another by skin and silence, just as dust is not impenetrable and the message of sticks can be interpreted after hours of intimacy. But in the presence of Brendan Boyle, the German was the victim of his European, or even his human inheritance. (*Voss* 170)

The blacks are not really human — Voss's 'human inheritance', forced upon him by Boyle's presence, stands between him and the Aborigines. This is to repeat a metaphor that has done a great deal of political and ideological work in Australia, even more than in other settler-colonial states. The notion that indigenous peoples belong more to nature than to humanity has helped discount their prior claims to the country. Which is to say that White's primitivist use of Aboriginality in *Voss* is doing the work of what is often called 'colonial discourse' — the set of ideas and descriptions of indigenous peoples that smoothed the way for their conquest and naturalised their subjugation.

Yet this point is a little simple, because White is not himself a humanist but a modernist transcendentalist. For him, 'being human' is not a value in itself; when all is said and done, white 'civilisation' is empty, inauthentic. So, when Voss wants to communicate with blacks as if he were communing with nature, he is looking to engage in a 'deeper' mode of communication than is possible in conversation with other whites. Like the landscape, the Aborigines represent a glimpse of that primordial, non-human order for which Voss is searching. Voss may fail, he may be motivated by an ambition to become more like a god than a man, but this does not mean that the reader is supposed to accept the all-too-human society and values from which he flees.

When he is introduced to the Aborigines, Voss's mysticism grips him, and, honouring the traditions of European explorers, he gives Dugald, the older Aboriginal man, a brass button:

The old man was very still, holding the token with the tips of his fingers, as if dimly aware in himself of an answer to the white man's mysticism. He could have been a thinking stick, on which the ash had cooled after purification by fire, so wooden was his old scarified, cauterised body, with its cap of grey, brittle ash. Inside the eyes moved some memory of myth or smoke.

> The youth, on the other hand, had been brought to animal life. Lights shone in his skin, and his throat was rippling with language. He was giggling and gulping. He could have eaten the brass button. (*Voss* 170–1)

That 'memory of myth or smoke' in a man whose body has become a 'thinking stick' stands in contrast to the somewhat Europeanised and corrupted Jackie who wants — literally — to consume the button, as if he has not reached the cultural level at which 'consumption' of goods is to be taken metaphorically. What is not given to either character is a sense of Aboriginal society and culture on its own terms. To describe the contents of Dugald's consciousness vaguely as 'some memory of myth or smoke' is to use him as a figure of the W/white anxiety that the cultural coherence myth can offer has disappeared from modernity, all the more so because it has merely become 'some memory' in Aborigines. It is always in the coloniser's interests to forget that colonised peoples' traditions endure.

White describes pre-contact Aboriginal societies and cultures a little more fully in two later scenes in *Voss* as well as in *A Fringe of Leaves*, the novel in which White retells the story of Eliza Fraser, the woman who was shipwrecked on Fraser Island in 1836 and briefly lived among the indigenous people. Leaving aside the (postcolonial) question of whether a white can offer culturally sensitive representations of such situations at all, in each case the writing confidently glides over an obvious lack of knowledge about Aboriginal life-ways. In *Voss*, Dugald is entrusted with Voss's letter back to the settlement, but meets some of his own people, and does not deliver it. The description of the meeting of Aborigines has a strangely conventional heterosexual eroticism, as if the hundreds of colonial soft-core descriptions of 'native' women's nakedness are, for the moment, controlling White's writing:

> He came to a lake in which black women were diving for lily roots. In the dreamlike state he had entered, it seemed natural that these women should be members of his own tribe, and that they should be laughing and chattering with him as he squatted by the water's edge, watching their hair tangle with the stalks of lilies, and black breasts jostle the white cups. (*Voss* 219)

And when Dugald and his 'tribe' destroy the letter they do so for reasons that fit into a certain white interpretation of Aboriginal customs:

the tribe think the letter is an expression of thoughts that might materially hurt them. The belief that writing possesses magical powers is not being ridiculed here (White himself shared it); but these Aborigines, some of whom are familiar with white ways, lack a savviness that their victors are assumed to possess.

These problems are still more apparent in *A Fringe of Leaves*, where, for instance, the physician conjurer who draws a stone from the dead child's mouth comes straight out of Fenimore Cooper (*FL* 261). By this time, though, a disjuncture between White's role as a (postcolonial) public intellectual and as a novelist is apparent. *A Fringe of Leaves* was written alongside a campaign to save Fraser Island from sand mining, in the course of which White paid for an archaeologist to go to the island to uncover its Aboriginal past. An anthropologist he consulted could find no records of Fraser Island Aboriginal rituals, so White's Aborigines simply fit into the narrative to meet Ellen's spiritual needs (*Life* 551). When, at the novel's climax, she joins in a rite involving the eating of human flesh, it becomes a kind of sacrament, a gesture of passing over into another culture. To Ellen, the 'cannibal feast' has 'something akin to the atmosphere surrounding communicants coming out of church looking bland and forgiven after the early service' (*FL* 271). The scene is conceptualised in terms not unlike that of Roger Caillois's famous essay on festival, first published in Bataille's journal *Documents*, in which controlled transgression stabilises social cohesion:

> In a totemic society, sexual and dietary sacrilege . . . aim at guaranteeing food and fertility for the group during a new time period. License is tied to the ceremony newly reviving the sacred animal or to the one integrating young people into the adult society . . . These rites . . . constitute a return to chaos.[7]

But Ellen must forget that she has shared this 'abomination of human behaviour'. White uses cannibalism to insist upon Australia's lack of public ceremonies, its failure to recognise tragic, transgressive drives, and hence its fragmentation. But, paradoxically, White's critique of modern Australia made it harder for him to imagine pre-contact Aboriginal society except in the historically most loaded of all Western primitivist categories — the cannibal.

What about White's representation of urban Aborigines? Alf Dubbo in *Riders in the Chariot* represents his most sustained attempt to describe a contemporary Koori. This time White does not mould the past into primitivist categories, but pictures the present in terms of the period's social policies. In this novel he was gripped by that form of spiritual syncretism in which all religious/mystical traditions were reduced to a single 'perennial philosophy' — to cite the title of Aldous Huxley's book, which, along with the republication of Jung's works, helped to popularise the syncretist movement during the 1950s. For syncretism, what counts finally is less the difference between certain spiritual traditions than their convergence — dramatised in *Riders in the Chariot* by four characters from various ethnic backgrounds, all having the same vision of the Chariot. Because Alf is a seer of the Chariot too, his Aboriginality is much more a matter of his being the victim of everyday racism than of any core of Aboriginal belief. In historical terms, his lack of his own cultural roots underpins his availability for syncretism, working in the spirit of the assimilationist policies that held sway until 1965.

Yet White is writing at the end of the assimilationist era, and the text betrays certain anxieties about the way its own syncretism is erasing Alf's people's culture. White writes this passage from Alf's point of view:

When the white man's war ended, several of the whites bought Dubbo drinks to celebrate the peace, and together they spewed up in the streets, out of stomachs that were, for the occasion, of the same colour. At Rosetree's factory, though, where he began to work shortly after, Dubbo was always the abo. Nor would he have wished it otherwise, for that way he could travel quicker, deeper, into the hunting grounds of his imagination.

The white men had never appeared pursier, hairier, glassier, or so confidently superior as they became at the excuse of peace. As they sat at their benches at Rosetree's, or went up and down between the machines, they threatened to burst right out of their singlets, and assault a far too passive future. Not to say the suspected envoys of another world. (*RC* 371)

The racism of which Alf is a victim strengthens his capacity to see whiteness not as norm but as hegemony (even the war is the 'white man's war'), and to look at white, heterosexual masculinity, in particular, with a disenchanted eye. By being positioned as an 'abo' he can maintain and explore his difference privately; he can resist assimilation and join that tiny community of seers scapegoated by Anglo society. Explore what difference? In the passage Alf's deep interiority is presented only fleetingly, in the trite and sentimental metaphor 'the hunting grounds of his imagination', and that imagination produces Western art. Alf is neither of the white world nor of his own world — which has vanished. This state of exile in his own country is so crippling that he ends up by playing Peter the betrayer to Himmelfarb's Christ; Himmelfarb, as Jewish, at least does possess a living tradition. Yet the important point is not so much that the novel's structuration of character mirrors an early postcolonial politics of ethnicity, but that nothing in Dubbo's Aboriginality is affirmed as part of Australia's future.

Yet one needs to be careful in judging White's failure here too quickly: the politics of postcolonial white and Aboriginal cultural relations remain complex. To insist on the difference between the two sides is liberating (in that it begins to affirm Aboriginal culture on its own terms) but it is also imprisoning (in that it limits both sides to maintaining separate traditions, and may underemphasise the ways in which both 'cultures' have interacted since contact). The difficulty, though, is that White could not engage even this postcolonial problematic. For him Aboriginals were finally another outsider group, but one without surviving traditions, compelled, at best, to universal spiritual experiences that may sometimes be read as blocked versions of his own vocation. From a fully fledged postcolonial perspective, White's representations of indigenous peoples show that the Australia he returned to, and wrote of and for, was not quite the Australia of the future.

3 THE CULTURAL CRITIC

Although White did not write novels simply to comment on society, he belonged to a modernist literary movement that can only be understood in terms of its critique of contemporary culture. This is not to say that his fictions are critical essays in disguise, but that his novels' contents and values, and to some extent their techniques, are motivated by a conscious and mainly adversarial attitude to the society he lived in. Even his claims for art's special aura and his enthusiasm for the notion of genius continually refer back to his diagnosis of modern society. This should not surprise us. Historically the idea that art's beauty and power are jeopardised by the dirty work of critique emerges from a radical judgement of society. Art's autonomy, its independence from the political, was only affirmed because most other social forms were rejected. For most of his career, White still belonged to this aestheticist-modernist tradition.

In this chapter I want to describe the ways that White judged society in his writings. I will continue to argue, conventionally enough, that his critiques turn around a distinction between serious art and banal culture that allows him to suppose that great art has spiritual qualities of its own. But I also want to extend the argument that the spiritual and the aesthetic have unstable relations in White's work, that one does not underpin the other.

Let us remember, just to start, that White made a point of giving superficial characters good taste: for instance, one of his silly women, the Princess in *The Eye of the Storm*, like White himself, admires Stendhal and Odilon Redon and despises the middlebrow writers Paul Bourget and Henry Bataille. After *The Solid Mandala*, aestheticism's promise certainly fades for White, even in *The Vivisector*, which on the surface seems secure in its faith in artistic genius. A key scene indicates the beginnings of White's recantation: the moment, early in *The Solid*

Mandala, when the Brown twins act a play for their parents. Waldo, the young would-be writer and aesthete, presents a 'Greek tragedy', while his brother Arthur pretends to be a cow. There is no doubt that Arthur's cow is more moving than Waldo's tragedy, the message being that the classics lack values in themselves. What is important is Arthur's innocence: his spirituality, in a word. But this transference from aesthetic culture to spiritual values is hard for White to sustain. His later works, notably *The Twyborn Affair*, begin to move away from the transcendentalism of modernist cultural criticism towards what is sometimes called a 'postmodernism', no longer confident of its ability to appeal either to art or the spirit as grounds for secure values or sanctioned insights. Here, an individual's life is reduced to a series of roles, a parade of pleasures and pains, memories and anticipations, without deep reach or coherence.

The most striking feature of White as a cultural critic is that he has no positive sense of society, let alone the state. Unlike European realists such as George Eliot or Tolstoy, his most serious characters rarely find their purpose within norms offered to them by the communities they are born into. And, because he hardly ever describes the most important organisations through which modern society reproduces itself, his novels present a peculiarly restricted range of social fields.

As we have seen, White's return to Australia after the war marked an ambivalent rejection of the global metropolitan centres with their deeply embedded social structures and material cultures. This also meant that, especially after *The Living and the Dead*, his novels were not quite set in the contemporary world. They rarely take place in factories or offices. His characters hardly ever read newspapers or listen to the radio, and when they do these are trivial experiences. They don't drive cars (nor, revealingly, did White himself). So, in White's novels, the flow of administered and commodified everyday life, with its dependence on policing, managerialism, entertainment, advertising, driving, welfare and so on, exists in the background; it forms a dull hum against which moral and aesthetic judgements may be made and an individual's emotional and spiritual longings enacted. The only real exception to this absence of modern industrialised and disciplined culture is the movies, and it is there, as we will see, that certain key scenes in White's novels occur.

The banality of everyday modern life

White knew that he was badly equipped to chronicle everyday modern life. What he called its 'banality' overwhelmed him. As he put it in a letter written while he was revising *The Eye of the Storm*:

> I am now about two-thirds of the way through the second version of the novel: hating it at present; every word is a stone to be lifted painfully. I find it increasingly hard to convey ordinary objects (a telephone, say) or necessary moves (from one room to another) without being overwhelmed by the banality they have in everyday life — and particularly Australian everyday life. (*Letters* 391)

From the perspective of the modernist cultural critic à la White, this banality is not a property of things like telephones, but of the systems to which they belong, which damage individual dignity. Modern systems and markets de-individuate and de-spiritualise people. By the mid-1950s, White predictably saw the US as the centre of modern banality. His comments about the country during a 1958 visit were characteristic: 'it is a horrifying kind of sub-civilisation, full of sudden gusts of fascism. The routine of living has been made so easy that the average person has lost touch with life, its primary forms and substances' (*Life* 341).

Earlier he had regarded London much the same way. *The Living and the Dead*, for instance, begins with a passage that could have come from D. H. Lawrence:

> Outside the station, people settled down again to being emotionally commonplace. There was very little to distinguish the individual feature in the flow of faces. Certainly it was night, but even where a wave of neon washed across the human element, it uncovered no particular secret, just the uniform white, square or oblong, tinged for a moment with the feverish tones of red or violet. (*LD* 7)

Here, the London tube and streets are peopled by faceless, ugly crowds, deprived of strong emotions. The passage seems like a typical modernist rejection of the massification and abstraction of modern life. Soon, however, it turns into something deeper, less a denunciation of 'mass-man' than a constellation of expressionist portraits:

The light that touched him [Elyot Standish], the street lights that have no respect for the personal existence, shaved his face down to the bones, left it with the expression of the street faces. The sockets of his eyes were dark. Two empty saucers in the bone. He remembered the face of the German woman, moments earlier on the platform, resting on her husband's shoulder in a last unseeing embrace. Or rather, you were drawn beyond the eyes of the little German Jewess into a region where the present dissolved, its forms and purpose, became a shapeless, directionless well of fear. (*LD* 7)

The way in which public spaces project people into a kind of death in life dissolves into a recognition of the concrete historical tragedy of the Nazi ethnocides. Indeed throughout the novel, White's rejection of modern life reaches beyond that of earlier European modernists such as Lawrence or Woolf. For them, contemporary life de-individualises and banalises; at its most extreme (as in their representations of the First World War) modernity can manufacture human death. White's point, however, is that the 'ease' and affluence of modern (Americanised) life, which cuts people off from authentic existence, requires violence, sacrifice and scapegoating; in those 'gusts of fascism', normal people feed off the fear they create in their victims. I will return to this.

Film

To examine White's cultural critique in more detail we need to separate his diagnosis of contemporary everyday life from his solutions. There is no better place to begin than at the movies. Like the first-generation anglophone modernist writers (Joyce is a partial exception), White thought of literature as a different category from industrialised media such as cinema. This is already a sign of his old-fashionedness: the convergence between high and low culture was well under way among avant-garde groups in France by the 1920s, and arguably the most successful of all postwar novels in the high modernist tradition — Malcolm Lowry's *Under the Volcano* — consciously grafted filmic narrative techniques onto the novel form.

But White was less adventurous. Although in real life he had a fascinated familiarity with Hollywood, for a long time he was unable to recognise the potential for exchange between the two forms. For him, film still threatened values upheld by serious literature. This changed somewhat in the 1960s, when there were serious efforts to film *Voss*, and White became involved enough to want to have a say in deciding the project's actors and directors (*Letters* 442). He wrote *A Fringe of Leaves* (1976) — his most conventional and middlebrow text — with a movie (and then an opera) adaptation in mind, and two years later was directly involved in movie production with the unsuccessful *The Night the Prowler*.

Just because high literature was supposed to have a radically different value from commercial cinema, references to film became an important means through which White could define and imagine characters, especially in the novels written in the late 1950s and early 1960s (a period when critiques of so-called 'mass culture' were themselves mass-produced). In *Riders in the Chariot*, Mrs Jolley, one of those profoundly malevolent middle-aged women characters strewn across his work, goes to the movies to confirm her 'belief' in the importance of 'being a lady'.

> She preferred to believe, however, and so Mrs Jolley would go to the pictures. To sit at the pictures sucking a lolly — not a hard one — after dropping the paper, along with memories and intentions, under the seat, was to indulge in sheerest velvet. It was a pity, though, about the hard lollies; the smell of a hot, moist caramel almost drove her nuts. But she would sit, and the strangest situations would pass muster as life. That lean young fellow, in crow's-feet and leather pants, might just have reached down, and put his hand — it made her lolly stick; and Ava and Lana, despite proportions and circumstances, could have been a couple of her own girls. Best of all was a picture about a mother. She knew by heart the injustices to expect, not to mention the retribution, so that, at the end, the wurlitzer rising from its well only completed her apotheosis. When she smelled the *vox humana*'s rose and violet breath, and felt the little hammers striking on her womb, then she was, indeed, fulfilled. (*RC* 44)

This is a crucial passage in that it points directly towards the novel's finale: Mrs Jolley's 'apotheosis' at the movie's end is a dark and banal anticipation of Himmelfarb's death. Mrs Jolley will help to bring about Himmelfarb's crucifixion, and in this extraordinarily condescending scene her cruelty is given some motivation. She responds to the movies erotically: the sticky lolly that softens her up to imagine the star putting his hand down into her is a (misogynist) figure for female genital sexuality — a connection all the more intense because Mrs Jolley's husband is dead, and her non-fantasy sex life null. She can only forget her husband when the movie ends and the music 'strikes her womb'. Whatever else it may be, her will to evil is positioned here as unsatisfied female sexual desire. She will help kill Himmelfarb out of revenge for her own loss, and from within a dream world that Hollywood helps manufacture.

In this way, Mrs Jolley's psychology helps to support, and is supported by, a set of more abstract cultural-political values. Whereas Himmelfarb is a student of ancient Jewish mystical and ethical traditions as set down in the Kabbalah and Torah, Mrs Jolley is a fan of contemporary movie-fantasies. Himmelfarb's tradition requires asceticism and learning, hers this kind of sticky pleasure, where lollies, stars and genitals overflow into one another.

The gender difference goes further here than may at first appear: the passage adheres to the wider cultural logic by which women are consistently placed alongside passively received 'mass culture' against actively engaged 'high culture'. The relative value of these cultural forms, as the text insists we regard them, is most powerfully articulated in Mrs Jolley's notion that 'Ava and Lana, despite proportions and circumstances, could have been a couple of her own girls'. Ava is Ava Gardner, Lana, Lana Turner, two major 'sex symbols' of the late 1940s and early 1950s. Both lived fast, troubled lives (they shared a husband, the band-leader Artie Shaw — one of seven spouses, in Turner's case) and indeed, at the time when White was beginning to think about his novel, Turner was in the headlines because her daughter had stabbed her lover to death.

The point is that these stars are not at all like Mrs Jolley's girls, who live petit-bourgeois suburban Australian lives, and that Hollywood's danger is precisely that it allows the 'strangest situations to pass muster as life'. Which only goes to show again that, despite appearances, the Kabbalah is much more livable, more realistic than Hollywood. Himmelfarb's death represents the murder of a spiritual tradition that respects effort and strict borders by a manufactured dream in which anything goes and reality is lost.

My second example of White's representation of movie-going comes from a time when it had become more difficult to uphold art against popular cinema. In *The Vivisector*, Hurtle Duffield goes to the movies with his friend and sexual partner Nance, who is a prostitute:

> Again the long sad picture had got possession of her [Nance]. That was what she wanted: to be slowly and sadly possessed by a lost marquise in crushed organdie. And what he wanted was not the common possessive pross he loved by needful spasms, but to shoot at an enormous naked canvas a whole radiant chandelier waiting in his mind and balls. (*V* 207)

This is bad writing, in that it crudely repeats the stereotypes in which the division between high art and low culture has been gendered. But neither the novel nor this passage is wholly fixed in this false opposition. After all, Hurtle finds a love and acceptance with Nance that is barely available to him elsewhere. In fact, this moment when they share different movie experiences allows Hurtle's ambitions as an artist and Nance's emotional needs to be joined rather than separated. Oddly enough, it is the screen's sheer size that joins them; its hugeness allows them to eroticise it. Each takes the erotic relation to the screen in a different direction: Nance, a cultural dupe, imagines herself possessed by an aristocrat; Hurtle, the artist, imagines himself, Renoir-like, ejaculating paint at a screen that he has transformed into an 'enormous naked canvas'. It is a revealing passage because, even though it relies on the standard, gendered opposition between Hollywood and high art, it also undoes that opposition. Hurtle's high aesthetic ambitions are, in this moment, as derivative and as reliant on the screen as Nance's romance-identifications. Because both are finally responses to the giant screen's power, White's artist's grand aesthetic project becomes as much — or as little — a fantasy as his prostitute's cheap romanticism.

White's society

Hurtle and Nance and their differences take us more deeply into White's cultural critique. I have argued that he was unable to affirm the value of society as such, and an important reason for this should now begin to be clear. For White, modern society is not a unity: it is fundamentally divided, especially into class and gender groups, which indelibly mark most (but not all) individuals. As a field of essential differences, society cannot ground individual lives; an individual's class and gender position overrides more widely shared cultural traits or resources.

White's sense of class and his own class position are extremely important to his work and career. For most of his career, he is able to write inside the modernist-novel genre developed by British writers such as Lawrence or E. M. Forster because for him, like them, class differences remain insurmountable. White's novels, broadly speaking, place their characters into three class categories. First the rich, who, especially if they are young women (like Madeleine in *The Tree of Man*, Boo Hollingrake in *The Vivisector* or the young Mrs Hunter of *The Eye of the Storm*), are cut off from others by a golden narcissism; empty inside, as their sexual appeal fades, they become merely domineering. The second category is the *petite bourgeoisie* who (again, especially the women) are dominated by a crippling snobbishness: for instance, in *A Fringe of Leaves*, Mrs Merivale is dazzled by her friend Miss Scrimshaw's 'connection with the Honourable Mrs Chetwynd of Saffron Waldon' (*FL* 12). White's critique (or rather, hatred) of these characters is expressed by the way that he not only makes them less intelligent, less sensitive, less interested in a wider culture than other characters, but also provides them with less interiority, so much so that in *A Fringe of Leaves* or *The Solid Mandala* they serve merely as a chorus.

Then there is the working class. In White's novels working men and women are characteristically enveloped in their subordinate position, though this does not mean that he regards servants or working people as necessarily inferior. If anything (romantically), the contrary. The view from below, from the position of the 'humble', is as necessary to many of his novels as it is to Virginia Woolf's *To the Lighthouse* or, in a different way, to Lawrence's *Sons and Lovers*, or indeed to Joyce's *Ulysses*. A character like Mrs Godbold in *Riders in the Chariot* represents a stability, an earthiness, that richer and more educated characters cannot achieve, or can only achieve at the cost of their reason, like Miss Hare in the same novel or Theodora Goodman in *The Aunt's Story*. At certain key moments White, like the British modernists, stabilised his value system by imagining and affirming working-class characters as less open to change and to identity crises — that is, to the forces of history — than the rich or educated.

By the 1930s this appeal to the working class had already become clearly politicised in White's predecessors. Art-novelists presented working-class characters who, in their nobility, bore the promise of the labour movement. But workers were also eroticised by writers such as D. H. Lawrence in *Lady Chatterley's Lover* and E. M. Forster in *Maurice*. This 'eroticism of the oppressed', as we can call it, actually ran counter to left-wing culture. Nobody could be further from the labour movement than D. H. Lawrence, for instance. It would be too cynical to suggest that the joys of rough trade required the 'rough' to stay rough; it is more that these novelists set erotic and vitalist values in opposition to the political demand for social justice. Labour could be sexualised to the extent that it was not conceded political agency.

White's *The Living and the Dead* treats this tension crudely enough. Elyot, White's approximate *alter ego* in the novel, has a grandfather who was a traditional working-class radical in what the narrator dismissively calls 'a concentration of theory' — echoing a critique of working-class aspirations expressed as long ago as the late eighteenth century by Edmund Burke (*LD* 21). On the other hand, both Elyot and his sister Eden fall in love with a worker–hero, Joe Barnett, who dies in the Spanish Civil War. And the novel champions their love and desire quite explicitly against politics. As Eden says, in a big speech with all the weight of the narrative behind it:

> I believe, Joe, but not in the parties of politics, the exchange of one party for another, which isn't any exchange at all. Oh, I can believe, as sure as I can breathe, feel, in the necessity for change. But it's a change from wrong to right . . . I can believe in right as passionately as I have it in me to live . . . I want to unite those who have the capacity for living, in any circumstance, and make it the one circumstance. I want to oppose them to the destroyers, to the dealers in words, to the diseased, to the most fatally diseased — the indifferent. (*LD* 253–4)

Here capacity to live becomes, if not quite to a Lawrentian degree, a capacity to have and invite desire, to be sexual. Joe Barnett's cause is good, not as a cause, but because the energy with which he enters it is so closely bound to his erotic glamour.

The flip side of the sexually vital worker is the good servant figure, who is required to keep class categories in place. In *The Living and the Dead*, White can write of Julia Fallon, a solid, dependable nurse — a type who will become part of his repertoire and be most fully treated in *The Eye of the Storm*:

> She had all the integrity, the dignity, the directness of a Flemish primitive. Watching her grave, slow movements with the child, there was an absorption in them that reassured . . . Ungainly perhaps. But you overlooked the ungainliness, as in the Flemish primitive, for the sake of economy and logic, and the effort that lends integrity. Julia took possession of the child. He became hers, in the way a child does. A child is always the possession, not of the mother, but of the nurse. (*LD* 58)

Here three textual figures — the narrator, the implied reader and the character having the thoughts — are (all too clumsily) placed in one class, Julia in another. This is possible rhetorically because she is simultaneously primitivised and aestheticised: she has the presence, not of a modern individual, but of the subject of an old Flemish painting à la Proust. Later in the novel, this value system becomes explicit when Elyot visits a working-class house. 'There were two countries, the countries of different moons, the different languages, intuitive and reasoned,' he says, in terms based on a famous passage from Benjamin Disraeli's novel *Sybil*, but twisted towards Lawrentian vitalism (*LD* 250). Here, quite simply, the working class relates to the bourgeoisie as intuition does to reason.

I would argue that White, like his British predecessors, could transfer moral characteristics such as humility and stability onto a class because he imagined one kind of work — service work, and especially servants' work — as typical of the class as a whole. In historical and sociological terms, this is ridiculous: one of the most important shifts in Western industrialised economies was the decline of live-in servant labour, especially after the First World War. Yet, like his older British peers, White confidently brings servants into his novels, and often heroicises them, Mrs Godbold of *Riders in the Chariot* being a good example. Of course, this is a direct result of his having been brought up in a household with servants. It is also one of the conditions underlying the belatedness of his narrative forms, his tendency to work in a vein much closer to British writers of the First World War than his American contemporaries. This is borne out by the fact that two of his early novels, *Happy Valley* and *The Tree of Man*, which do not contain heroicised servants, are written in a somewhat different narrative style from his later works. *Happy Valley*, in particular, owes more to American modernists such as Gertrude Stein, Sherwood Anderson, even Ernest Hemingway, who set out to construct simple characters through a pared-down prose aimed at clearing everything from their vision except the elemental conditions of existence. White turned to the British modernist model to sustain his novel-writing career past his initial responses to rural Australia — either negative (*Happy Valley*) or more positive (*The Tree of Man*).

The decisive point, however, is that all his novels imply readers who do not belong to the servant or working class that the novels spiritualise. The humble are always other to, and finally lesser than, the author and his readers (even if they are morally and spiritually superior). And when industrial workers enter White's novels, which they rarely do, they tend to be resentful, cruel and stupid, like the crowd that crucifies Himmelfarb in *Riders in the Chariot*.

Women

White's relation to women was complicated. As a homosexual who had identified himself as a so-called 'invert', he thought of himself as in part a woman. On the other hand, he also feared and was repulsed by femininity, especially in the form of motherhood. This ambivalent orientation imposes itself on White's cultural critique of gender and familial relations. The basic grounds of White's conceptualisation of femininity have already become apparent. They can be expressed at a very abstract level: for him, women do not preserve boundaries and autonomy: they are enveloping, fluid, capable — like old witches — of myriad transformations, and all because they are not quite complete in themselves. 'The fervid desire of a certain type of feminine mind to identify itself with objects, with nature, with art, drained the dignity from these,' as he puts it through Elyot Standish in a typical early statement (*LD* 179). This seems to be why there are, for instance, no women 'geniuses' in White's works.

This basic, almost ontological, conception of women is articulated at a particular moment in history. White wrote over a period when the politics of women's social position (for instance, the question of workplace equality) and of femininity (that is, images of what women should be) became increasingly unstable. Attacks on 'momism' were quite common in the 1940s, especially after Philip Wylie's best-seller *Generation of Vipers* (1942), but the postwar decade saw an orgy of celebration of women's place as mothers in the home. Then, in another turn, the postwar consensus on women's domestication fell apart from about 1963, the year of publication of Betty Friedan's *The Feminine Mystique*, which powerfully documented women's disillusion with their restricted role as homemakers. By the early 1970s, a consciously political women's movement had irrevocably shifted relations between the genders in the West.

The fear of women, and especially mothers, that runs through White's texts needs to be read in the light of the contested ideological structures that attempted to define femininity around maternity. For instance, his creation of characters such as Mrs Jolley was not just a sign of his own Oedipal struggle with motherhood, but represented an attack on one of the primary struts of Cold War conservatism, with its insistence that a good society relied on Mum doing her thing for her husband and the kids at home (though these values were so widespread that at the time they were barely considered conservative at all). The emphasis on the home and maternity in Cold War conservatism, in turn, needs to be read along two even more abstract axes. First, the 'free' world's emphasis on family and the home implicitly contrasted it with the Cold War enemy — communism — for which society as a whole, not the nuclear family, was the fundamental horizon of citizens' lives. Secondly, the theme of woman-as-primarily-domestic was partly driven by the marketing efforts of a host of industries producing goods for domestic space, notably the construction industry (which was busy building new suburban houses) and the consumer-durables industry (mass-producing furniture, washing-machines, fridges, radios, record-players, dishwashers and, not least, televisions). Feminism emerges as a force in the 1960s when, simultaneously, the communist threat recedes and these industries reach maturity in the market-place.

White does not deal with these historical structures explicitly, but they impinge upon his writings. In this context, his resistance to the supposed banality of modern consumerism works in the same direction as his negative pictures of mothers. Most notably, White's women are more secular, less spiritual than his men, in a little piece of ideology that fits the way in which the marketing of home-making was more directed at women than at men.

Another way of putting all this is that in White's novels women, like working-class characters, are placed at a distance from, are other to, the narrator and implied reader. This is one reason why even class categories are typified by women rather than men (in White's novels the truly typical suburban middle-class person is the wife rather than the husband — who has more possibility of jumping across social categories). It is true that, especially after the emergence of feminism, there are moments when the narrator takes on a woman's point of view against masculinity. In *The Eye of the Storm*, the nurse Flora Manhood disenchantedly watches men in a pub:

> On the other side men were standing watching an infringement of their rights. Whether pursy, beery-eyed blokes, of the type which crooks a finger at its schooner to establish this delicate relationship, or lean smoothies who show they know better by nursing a glass of pallid spirits, all were of the superior sex. (*ES* 551)

And then, without a blink, White shifts his narration from Flora's point of view to that of the anonymous working-class men, in a grotesque caricature of male chauvinist piggery (to use another phrase of the time):

> Nobody ever said you can do without a woman; who can even become a permanent asset: to throw the steak on the grill, iron the shirts and keep the home nice and neat. Wives are economic like; that's a different matter. As for this girl, showing too much of herself in the doorway, she didn't rate much above a back-seat fuck. (*ES* 551)

Obviously the reader is supposed to recoil from this, and yet the very banality of the sexism here reflects back onto Flora's incipient feminism. It is as if her view of men is like their view of her: both are limited. Here men and women act out, one more time, the age-old drama of miscommunication.

It is when White describes heterosexual sex in some detail that what is perhaps his most fundamental criticism of modern society emerges: that modern society — especially in its Australian form — is too dependent on the nuclear, heterosexual family, and on life as lived in family houses. Take this example from *The Twyborn Affair*, where a rich farmer's wife is seducing another of White's *alter egos*, Eddie Twyborn:

> He buckled his belt, which to some extent increased his masculine assurance, but it was not to his masculine self that Marcia was making her appeal. He was won over by a voice wooing him back into childhood, the pervasive warmth of a no longer sexual, but protective body, cajoling him into morning embraces in a bed disarrayed by a male, reviving memories of toast, chilblains, rising bread, scented plums, cats curled on sheets of mountain violets, hibiscus trumpets furling into sticky phalluses in Sydney gardens, his mother whom he should have loved but didn't, the girl Marian he should have married but from whom he had escaped, from the ivied prison of a tennis court, leaving her to bear the children who were her right and fate, the seed of some socially acceptable, decent, boring man.
>
> He was drawn back to Marcia by the bright colours of retrospect, the more sombre tones of remorse. He lowered his face into the tumult of her breasts. (*TA* 222)

Eddie is basically sexually interested in men, not women, and in this scene he finds it difficult to maintain desire. He can only have sex with Marcia through regressive memories that overflow with remorse for his unvanquishable horror of conventional family life. As Marcia's body becomes a mother's womb for him, it imprisons rather than envelops, so that his vague sexual repulsion is transformed into a quasi-political resistance to the social values and ways of life that the womb represents for him. Those values place individuals in fixed gender identities, limiting them to the 'decent, boring' lives whose hypocrisies and disavowals are hinted at by that strange phrase, 'the tumult of her breasts'. The false decency of conventional heterosexual life is here based on hiding the chaos of maternal being and desire.

Spirituality

As Eddie leaves Marcia after the scene just quoted, he rejects sexuality as a means for finding himself:

> In his own experience, in whichever sexual role he had been playing, self-searching had never led more than briefly to self-acceptance. He suspected that salvation most likely lay in the natural phenomena surrounding those unable to rise to the spiritual heights of a religious faith: in his present situation the shabby hills, their contours practically breathing as the light embraced them, stars fulfilled by their logical dowsing, the river never so supple as at daybreak, as dappled as the trout it camouflaged, the whole ambience finally united by the harsh but healing epiphany of cockcrow. (*TA* 223)

Rarely does White pose the connection between sexuality and spirituality more starkly than this. The search for 'salvation', directed at the Australian landscape, is motivated by the rejection of sexuality and the regimes that organise it as a means of self-knowledge. A similar narrative movement occurs in *The Tree of Man* when Stan, the novel's hero, has his epiphany just after he realises that his wife has had sex with a passing commercial traveller. But 'her importance had dwindled in the brilliance of the day'. Then a storm breaks:

> The man [Stan] who was watching the storm, and who seemed to be sitting right at the centre of it, was at first exultant. Like his own dry paddocks, his skin drank the rain. He folded his wet arms, and this attitude added to his complacency. He was firm and strong, husband, father, and owner of cattle. He sat there touching his own muscular arms, for he had taken off his shirt during the heat and was wearing his singlet. But as the storm increased, his flesh had doubts, and he began to experience humility. The lightning . . . had, it seemed, the power to open souls. It was obvious in the yellow flash that something like this had happened, the flesh had slipped from his bones, and a light was shining in his cavernous skull . . .

In his new humility, weakness and acceptance had become virtues. He retreated now, into the shelter of the veranda, humbly holding with his hand the wooden post that he had put there himself years before, and at this hour of the night he was quite grateful for the presence of the simple wood. As the rain sluiced his lands, and the fork of the lightning entered the crests of his trees. The darkness was full of wonder. Standing there somewhat meekly, the man could have loved something, someone, if he could have penetrated beyond the wood, beyond the moving darkness. But he could not, and in his confusion he prayed to God, not in specific petition, wordlessly almost, for the sake of company. Till he began to know every corner of the darkness, as if it were daylight, and he were in love with the heaving world, down to the last blade of wet grass. (*TM* 151)

Like the scene in *The Twyborn Affair*, this passage progresses away from sexuality to a love of nature as inhabited by God. Yet Stan's dismissal of his wife mimics her unfaithfulness. On the surface, the reader is being asked to accept that this religious act is more valuable, more profound, than Amy's sexual act — all the more so because this scene was based on an important event in White's own spiritual development (*Life* 282). But the transcendence of sexuality here is very compromised: the wooden post that Stan holds in his hands maintains a suggestion of autoeroticism, particularly as it provides an object for desire articulated in these terms: '[he] could have loved something, someone, if he could have penetrated beyond the wood'. It is because he cannot penetrate beyond the wood (as we might say, cannot fuck the wood) that he prays to God and falls in love with the 'heaving' world. What seems to be a progression from sexuality is in fact a displacement into another mode of sexuality, from heterosexual love to a form of fetishism, so that 'God' becomes the imagined spirit infusing the inanimate world as the object of sexualised desire. This is repeated in a more muted key, both in the scene quoted from *The Twyborn Affair* (when as Eddie leaves Marcia, the light 'embraces' the hill — as if Eddie projects nature having sex with itself) and in the eroticising of the Australian landscape in White's autobiography.

When he talked in public as a cultural critic, White thought about his spirituality in more conventional terms than this, as a question of 'faith', drawing on thinkers such as the Catholic existentialist Gabriel

Marcel, who meant a great deal to him. Writing to Clement Semmler in 1970 after finishing *The Vivisector*, he put it like this:

> I suppose what I am increasingly intent on trying to do in my books is to give professed unbelievers glimpses of their own unprofessed faith. I believe most people have a religious faith, but are afraid that by admitting it they will forfeit their right to be considered intellectuals ... The churches defeat their own aims, I feel, through the banality of their approach, and by rejecting so much that is sordid and shocking which can still be related to religious experience. (*Letters* 363)

A certain tendency towards transcendentalism and an acute sense of the insufficiency and fragmentariness of the everyday is rarely absent from White's work, but he was most explicitly concerned with mysticism in the period of his career that immediately follows his initial fame as a writer of genius — the period from *Riders in the Chariot* to *The Vivisector*. Leaving sexuality aside, it is possible to interpret White's spiritual orientations in terms of his ambition and the cultural demands made on him as an Australian 'great writer'. At one level, his mysticism was an attempt to consolidate and justify the seriousness with which he was being taken by critics and the media. Later critics have continued to argue that White's claim to greatness is to be found in his mysticism. David Tacey, for instance, has argued that White was a thoroughgoing Jungian, and that a detailed knowledge of Jung's esoteric and mystical archetypes is required for a full understanding of his work. It is a claim White himself rejected, writing of Tacey that 'he tries to tie his subject down in the strait jacket of his system and finds I don't fit. Of course I'm no expert on Jung, only picked up a few bits which suited my purpose, just as I've picked a few bits from Christian theology and the Jewish mystics' (*Letters* 566). In fact, *Riders in the Chariot* is the first and only book that even begins to deal systematically with a recognised mystical tradition (in this case, the Jewish tradition).

If White's mysticism was partly strategic, aimed at securing the seriousness of his work and reputation at a time when readings that analysed literature for its use of 'archetypal' images were fashionable among academic critics, he also turned to mysticism for technical reasons. It provided him with a means by which he could structure his novels. White's novels were not fundamentally plot-driven. Nor was he really a 'psychological' writer, primarily interested in the interplay of an individual consciousness and the world for its own sake, even in the few of his novels that concentrate on a single character's feelings and consciousness. This means that he often had difficulty in making his works achieve wholeness, or rather, a semblance of wholeness. Without the driving force of a strong story or a single, privileged consciousness, what principle might draw his texts' various incidents, their jumble of characters, together? One answer was a set of symbols that appear repeatedly in various contexts, tying characters and events to one another outside of any strong narrative or even psychological connection.

I am not arguing that these symbols have a merely organisational function in White's work. They are not simply and avowedly inserted into the work to provide unity. As we know, in some cases mystical moments inserted into his fictions apparently describe incidents drawn from his own life. In other cases they do draw upon a spiritual or cultural tradition and were aimed at spiritualising Australia. In fact, however, the way that White transfers spiritual epiphanies from his life to his novels, or attempts to work his fictional spiritualism on the world, also reveals the limits of such transferences and operations. Let us take one very obvious instance from *Riders in the Chariot*.

In this novel, four characters from different backgrounds all at some time experience a vision of riders in a chariot. Why riders in a chariot? What is the meaning of this vision, which is also a symbol? From which spiritual tradition does White inherit it? It turns out that White himself first encountered the riders in front of an art dealer's shop in up-market Bond Street in London. A painting by the French symbolist painter Odilon Redon was displayed in the window. The painting pictured Apollo, riding a chariot, killing Python — one of several images Redon painted on this Greek mythological theme. For Redon the image was an allegory symbolising art's victory over chaos, and more particularly, his own breakthrough into the use of colour, which followed a successful public auction of his work. He had taken the subject from Eugène Delacroix's famous ceiling painting in the Galerie d'Apollon in the Louvre (that holy shrine of aesthetic value), a daring borrowing that was an affirmation of Redon's ambition and confidence at the time.[1]

In terms of its immediate genealogy, then, White's *Riders in the Chariot* does not emerge from a spiritual or Christian tradition at all (despite the temptation to read it in terms of the four horsemen of the Apocalypse). It reaches back to an earlier moment of modern art, where it signifies art's will to power and order as well as modernist art's nascent market appeal. Redon's painting confirms high art's power as an institution, first via the image's capacity to claim harmony and completeness, and secondly via its capacity to form traditions. (A micro-tradition is brought into being by Redon's borrowing from Delacroix's ceiling painting, one that will be extended by White, and, fictionally, by Alf Dubbo, the artist-character who also knows Redon's image.) White's fictional characters see the riders in a spiritual experience, a cosmic illumination; indeed, by the massive coincidence that secures the novel's formal coherence, they each see the same vision independently. But the cultural history of the chariot that they see reveals that their shared spirituality refers less to the spirit than to art's will to power, not least in the market-place.

The technical, economic and aesthetic conditions of the transcendental here overwhelm its spiritual or lived function. For White, art (including music and fiction) is more effective than any social institution in affirming and communicating the spiritual. Art, however, cannot express spiritual illumination transparently: its highly structured forms are produced by individuals who must carefully find means to express themselves from within the technical and formal conventions that they inherit. Today (and long since) these conventions are far removed from spiritual or religious traditions, and only reach back to them under strain. Recognising this allows us to generalise the argument that White's characters' mystical moments are partly to be understood as technical requirements of the novels themselves (as well as expressing their author's ambitions). The slippage from the spiritual to the technical is an index of a larger cultural transformation, the way in which contemporary culture is grounded more on aesthetic forms, particularly fictions, than on religious or spiritual ones.

It is this that frustrates Himmelfarb, who, of all White's characters, is the one most securely trained within a mystical tradition:

he was racked by his persistent longing to exceed the bounds of reason: to gather up the sparks, visible intermittently inside the thick shells of human faces; to break through to the sparks of light imprisoned in the forms of wood and stone. Imperfection in himself had enabled him to recognise the fragmentary nature of things, but at the same time restrained him from undertaking the immense labour of reconstruction. So this imperfect man had remained necessarily tentative. He was for ever peering into bushes, or windows, or the holes of eyes, or, with his stick, testing the thickness of a stone, as if in search of further evidence, when he would have been gathering up the infinitesimal kernels of sparks, which he already knew to exist, and planting them again in the bosom of divine fire, from which they had been let fall in the beginning. (*RC* 141)

For Himmelfarb, another character who touches the ground a great deal, the divine sparks have been extinguished in a fallen world, imprisoned in objects. He cannot 'reconstruct' them from within his religious tradition — the implication being that only art can do that, in particular the art of the fiction in which he is a character. But, unlike the great texts of spiritual tradition, fictions are defined by their not being true, except in the most recondite of senses.

This returns us to White as a cultural critic. White's spirituality may be strategically and technically motivated; it may often represent a failed flight from dominant sexual regimes, or a relay from religion to fiction, but it also relies on what can be called a critical theory of social origins whose main point can be stated quite simply: society starts and continues in violence, human beings group together only by excluding and murdering their own. Thus kindness and warmth, what we can simply call goodness, is to be found in the victims and rejected. To take one example of many, in *Riders in the Chariot* it is the lesbian prostitute Hannah and the 'poofter' (White's word) Norm who take care of the young Aboriginal boy Alf Dubbo, when the respectable world has cast him out. In a sense White's critique of society — his rejection of community as a starting point for ethical and spiritual values as well as his emphasis on the *individual* genius — is part of his attempt to live and imagine a life without social violence. Here fictional imagining and faith in values seem to cohere. Rather than identifying with society, he identifies with those most exposed to that violence, among whom he includes the artist: 'throughout my life', he wrote to Ben Huebsch, 'I have been an outcast myself in one way and another: first a child with what kind of a strange gift nobody quite knew; then a despised colonial boy in an English public school; finally an artist in horrified Australia — to give you just a few instances' (*Letters* 180).

The account of society that valorises the outsider and scapegoat is basically, if not doctrinally, Christian. Human society is based on original sin; it reproduces itself through acts of treachery and murder, as Cain betrayed and murdered his brother Abel, and Christ was killed by the rich and powerful of his time. As we have seen, the Holocaust revitalised this sense of society in the late 1940s and 1950s. Apocalyptic imagery was everywhere, not least in the works of White's modernist painter friends, Francis Bacon and Roy de Maistre. By the end of his life at least, White had moved further: he was able not so much to place spirituality against society as to see transgression itself as enabling. Nowhere is there a clearer instance of this than in Ellen Roxburgh's act of cannibalism in *A Fringe of Leaves*, which she looks back on in these terms:

> Just as she would never have admitted to others how she had immersed herself in the saint's pool, or that its black waters had cleansed her of morbid thoughts and sensual longings, so she could not have explained how tasting flesh from the human thigh-bone in the stillness of a forest morning had nourished not only her animal body but some darker need of the hungry spirit. (*FL* 274)

Leaving aside the question of its primitivism, the difficulty with this passage is precisely that its transgressive solution to the shortcomings of everyday life belongs more to fiction than to life. In fact it is as if the filmic or operatic adaptation is already written into the cannibalism scene.

As both a cultural critic and a novelist, White offers glimpses of salvation in his texts, but these glimpses remain fictional, communicable only in films or novels or plays or operas. They can only establish themselves as more than fictional if society recognises White's novels and their values as central to its culture, as constitutive myths, we might almost want to say. If this has happened at all, it is at the level of lip-service, and for a tiny sector of the community as a whole. White is officially a genius, but remains more or less unread. Certainly the literal meanings of his texts — their spirituality and transgressive sexuality — have not been incorporated into public discourse. And one important reason why White is under-read is that, in his effort to create himself as a genius and to write culturally revivifying, deeply 'serious' fictions, he simplified and scapegoated ordinary life and people, most of all when they were heterosexual, middle-class women.

4   SEX AND THE FAMILY

Because White found it so difficult to affirm society either as a concept or as a set of institutions, sexual and familial relations are especially important in his writings. Among other things, his novels aim to work through his own family and sex life; to hurt or bind family members and lovers; to canvass new possibilities for intimate communities and sexual flows; and to lift the veil on conventional family ideals. The strongest element of his work is its ability to imagine characters connecting to each other in ways that distance his readers from the normative heterosexual family — and, more remarkably, from the prohibitions that sustain it, notably the prohibition on incest.

For White, the family is not a haven from uncontainable sexuality, nor a site of pure love. Sexuality within the family flows in all kinds of directions: from parents to children and back again, between brothers and sisters, between brother and brother. At the same time, social relations break down into astonishing moments of erotic intimacy and intensity. Attractions, gusts of emotion, bursts of insight flash out, as if society is an incestuous family writ large. And, if sex is potentially everywhere, so is hate: the one is the shadow of the other.

In picturing these erotic and aggressive flows, White is not urging his readers to reform modern family life. It is not as though he conceives some other kind of relation that might replace the current family, for instance. For him, as we have seen, sexuality is not, as it was for D. H. Lawrence, a ground on which to begin building a fuller existence, or even a good in itself. Because it is always underpinned by aggression, sex does not even seal intimacy; it is rarely a foundation for lasting connections. It is a gust, often causing shame: at best a 'lover' may become a habit. That is why White's fictional families often implode: siblings become sexual partners or share houses in new patterns of mutual neglect, love, dependency, nostalgia or repulsion.

These imploded families signal the impossibility of using sexuality or the family as a model for restructuring wider social relations, just as they demonstrate that early family life is the stage on which individuals' capacity to desire and individuate themselves is simultaneously shaped and limited.

The house

What is it that structures the family as it collapses under flows of desire and repulsion? A material thing — the family house, with the economic interests invested in it and the habits and memories that cling to it. White's houses often become not merely the setting but the content of his characters' lives. Here is Elyot Standish, returning home at the beginning of *The Living and the Dead*, remembering his dead mother's house:

> Perhaps because she had made it, an interior shaped and reshaped, the way a room can receive the imprint of its owner's life, even the first warning of death. The house, and particularly this room, had become almost the sole visible purpose of Mrs Standish's existence. And it continued to live in the inconclusive way of the houses of the dead. (*LD* 14)

In *The Eye of the Storm*, when her children winkle Mrs Hunter out of her house, they effectively kill her.

No doubt White's capacity to describe characters in terms of their houses had a great deal to do with his own class position. He came from a family associated with a particular house, Belltrees, and for him a house and where it is situated remained an important signifier of identity. But this emphasis on the family house is also a reflex of his genealogical position: as a homosexual who would never have children, he wrote as a family heir, not as a future ancestor. For him, living in a family house belonged to the past, not to the present or future.

White's family houses are tense places. On the one side, they are almost as close to those who live in them as their blood; on another, they provide the containment required to live an ordered life (like the various boxes and containers that litter his novels, but on a larger scale); on another still, they are prisons, concealing and silencing passions, and trapping those who live in them. It is no accident that the first Australian country house in his novels, Meroë of *The Aunt's Story*, has a name that signifies, among other things, 'country of bones' (*AS* 112). Here Theodora of *The Aunt's Story*, stuck at Meroë, talks about the house to her beloved niece Lou:

> She had told the story of Meroë, an old house, in which nothing remarkable had taken place, but where music had been played, and roses had fallen from their stems, and the human body had disguised its actual mission of love and hate. But to tell the story of Meroë was to listen also to her own blood, and, rather than hear it quicken and fail again, Theodora smoothed with her toe the light on the carpet, and said, 'But, my darling, there is very little to tell.' (*AS* 20)

The family house sets a stage on which its inhabitants adopt various disguises to elude the conventionally gendered and socialised selves on which parents insist, at least at one level. In the family house, beyond all transformation and theatre, a woman remains a grown little girl (literally so in cases like Miss Hare of *Riders in the Chariot*), a man a grown little boy. Yet certain travellers, passing by, can break open these identities. Sometimes such people without houses are figured as prophetic and liberated, other times as rootless and irresponsible: *The Aunt's Story* is written around the first structure, *The Tree of Man* around the second.

In *The Aunt's Story*, the tramp who passes through Meroë when Theodora is twelve anticipates, laconically enough, the path that her life will take after her mother's death when, at last, she leaves home:

> 'Yes,' said the man, 'it's as good a way of passing your life. So long as it passes. Put it in a house and it stops, it stands still. That's why some take to the mountains, and the others say they're crazy . . . And perhaps they're right. Though who's crazy and who isn't? Can you tell me that, young Theodora Goodman? I bet you couldn't.'
>
> He looked at her with a fierce eye, of which the fierceness was not for her.
>
> 'I would come if I could,' said Theodora.
>
> 'Yes,' said the man, 'You would.'
>
> 'Don't be silly,' said Fanny, 'You're a girl.' (*AS* 47)

This expresses with particular starkness one of the ways in which White structures relations between the family house and its children.

Life stops still in a house, congealed into false permanence by money and the security of a building. The mountains possess what the house lacks — true permanence, the capacity to endure without repression and exclusion.

Yet outside the house, on the road, there is the threat of craziness, whatever that means. Those who flee the house do so, most of all, because their gender and sexuality cannot be frozen or organised conventionally: Theodora (who as an adult has a moustache) is really not a 'girl' at all. 'I am a man,' she gets to say in the hallucinatory section of the novel set in a hotel in the south of France. And she is a man because her family's psychosexual dynamics push her to identify with her father. The family house congeals life, but it also jumbles identities. And vice versa: families push their members into becoming other to themselves, for the sake of rejecting a parent's authority; but families and parents lie waiting at the end of all flight and self-transformation, as the end of *The Twyborn Affair* makes clear.

For White, houses can more easily shelter authentic being in the world when they begin to rot away, as if reality can be most effectively encountered and accepted in the cracks in the walls, the overgrown gardens. White's most sustained description of the decayed mansion comes in *Riders in the Chariot*, where the saintly idiot, Miss Hare, lives on in Xanadu after her parents' deaths:

> Long after her father was dead, and disposed of under the paspalum of Sarsaparilla, and the stone split by sun and fire, with lizards running in and out of the cracks, Miss Hare acquired something of the wisdom she had denied possessing the night of the false suicide. Sometimes she would stump off into the bush in one of the terrible jumpers she wore of brown ravelled wool, and an old stiff skirt, and would walk, and finally sit, always listening and expecting until receiving. Then her monstrous limbs would turn to stone, although her thoughts would sprout in tender growth of young shoots, or long loops of insinuating vines, and she would glance down at her feet, and frequently discover fur lying there from the throes of some sacrifice. If tears ever fell then from her saurian eyes, and ran down over the armature of her skin, she was no longer ludicrous. She was quite mad, quite contemptible, of course, by standards of human reason, but what have those proved to be? (*RC* 37)

As the house and its surroundings decay, curious transformations and exchanges occur. Miss Hare has such a gift for passivity, for 'listening and expecting', that she seems not quite a human agent. Her clothes are a metaphor for this gift: her jumper of 'brown ravelled wool' already belongs to the bush. And this metaphor, at least for a moment, provides a bridge into larger social forms still. It is as if Miss Hare's passive naturalness is proper to a colonial economy so bound to the land and sheep. When the event that she awaits happens — her father's death — Miss Hare's body becomes like the house ('her monstrous limbs would turn to stone') and her mind metamorphoses into the vegetation that is creeping the house back into nature: 'her thoughts would sprout in . . . long loops of insinuating vines'. More than that: nature already contains the cruel psychodynamics that constitute society. Miss Hare's transformation into the bush happens at sites of 'sacrifice'. This scene, located in the grounds of Xanadu, presents a place to live in that is the very opposite of a box-like, falsely permanent materialisation of parental and social order. While Miss Hare becomes a house in decay and the house in decay becomes her, she is being prepared for her mystical illumination, her vision of the riders in the chariot. In this novel the struggle between forces of good and evil is figured (among other things) as the struggle between the brick suburban dwellings favoured by Mrs Jolley and Mrs Flack, and the versions of homelessness shared by Miss Hare, Alf Dubbo the Aboriginal artist, and Himmelfarb the wandering Jew.

Fathers

In chapter 3 I argued that families have played a specific role in Australian culture because, in the absence of more complex collective institutions early in the settlement period, two metropolitan social forms flourished: heterosexual families and male-centred sociability (so-called 'mateship'). Structurally, fathers lived at the borders of these two formations, in a split position that weakened them in relation to their children. Inside the family and in relation to ideals of masculinity centred on being a mate, they were somewhat emasculated; outside the family, it was difficult for their children, even their sons, to have access to dad-as-a-mate.

White's relationship with his father was organised through these larger structures, all the more so because his mother seems to have actively discouraged Patrick from ever becoming one of the boys: as we know, both as a child and as a novelist he remained involved in maternal fantasies and theatrics. White's identification with his writing self and his mother was so strong that when he set out to be an author he insisted on writing under the name Patrick Withycombe, his mother's maiden name, but his father would give him an allowance only if he wrote as Patrick White (*Life* 136). One can imagine few stronger attempts at what Lacanian psychoanalysts call 'repudiation of the paternal signifier'.

In White's fictions, fathers, if not literally absent, lack agency in their children's lives. It is not as if there are no warm father–child relations in the novels: in *The Aunt's Story*, for instance, Theodora loves and idealises her father, and White could describe the old man Holstius, whom she hallucinates at the end in Taos, as a 'delusion arising out of Theodora's love for her father' (*Life* 243). But, compared with mothers, fathers barely exist — even Holstius springs up out of Theodora's imagination because her father is *not* a strong figure in her life.

For psychoanalysis, this absence is to be read as an expression of desire: from its point of view, White wrote texts with such weak or absent fathers because he was acting out, at the level of fiction or fantasy, a wish to wipe his father away. Certainly his fictions over and over again tell what Freud called the family-romance narrative, fantasies in which children imagine they aren't their parents' children at all. Hurtle of *The Vivisector* is the clearest such case, and White called himself an 'ugly duckling' — identifying with a fairytale that crystallises the family-romance story. But White's negation of the father is better interpreted, in my opinion, as the expression of specific historical and familial conditions than as the work of unconscious desire, and is only describable in the most general terms through psychoanalytic theory.

White's inability or refusal to take the paternal position did not lead to any personal abjection or unravelling: on the contrary, he became a writer by not becoming a father and, as much as was possible, by not accepting the law of the father — that is, by rejecting both the established conventions of the society into which he was born and a place in the patrilineal chain. We can even say that he moves away from the paternal position most effectively by figuring himself as partly a woman, and then by elaborating a theory of sexed identity in general as an assemblage of different selves, each able to be acted out on different occasions (like Eddie Twyborn or the hero of his lost early novel 'Nightside'). He also moved away from the paternal position by rejecting the duties and interests of the Anglo-colonial establishment to which his family belonged. On the other hand, he did attempt to take on a displaced form of paternal rigidity through his intense investment in moral integrity (his fierce claims to stand for 'truth') and his somewhat less intense investment in art and art-literature with transcendental, organic unity as its aesthetic principle, which, in White's own terms, stands against the feminine.

Another relation to the father does occasionally emerge in White's texts. In *The Vivisector*, the young Hurtle's aesthetic gaze is formed when he first visits the rich Courtney family:

> Everything at Courtney's had a look of new. Even the banana tree. The dead leaves must have been picked off; the live ones might have been varnished. The rubbish bins shone like silver. The banana tree was swelling and fruiting, very purple. He was reminded of his own paler one. Then of Pa's wrinkled-looking, ugly old cock. (*V* 22)

Here Hurtle's incipient aestheticism, the force that will make an artist of him, is a product of a libidinal associative flow that returns to his father's penis in a horror that in turn — the possibility cannot be discounted — may mask incestuous desire. The ugliness beneath the rich, beautiful glossiness of the Courtneys' house is more than the effect of Hurtle's unbidden memory of his father's cock: it is a moral reminder of the limits of the Courtneys' money, the ultimate superficiality of what money can buy.

Indeed that 'wrinkled-looking' cock comes to be associated with the very stuff of Hurtle's art: light itself. In a classic journey out of the mother-centred, 'cultured' family-world towards the masculine public sphere and workplace, Hurtle goes with his (adopted) father to visit the family farm. When they arrive, his father says:

'Fine sheep country, son. You wanter keep yer eyes open, and you'll pick up a wrinkle or two.'

He was speaking as though Maman didn't exist, nor the painting by Boudin, nor the shelves of leatherbound books: when you knew all about them. Nor did he realise all the wrinkles you were picking up, not from the boring old sheep country, but from the world of light as the sun rose pale out of the hills, and the streams of liquid light were splashed across the white paddocks: from the sheep too, the wrinkled sheep, huddling or trudging. (*V* 104–5)

The word 'wrinkle', repeated more often than is tactful, moves quickly across the surface of these passages, describing his father's penis, then light, then sheep — at which point it acquires more buried meanings. For Hurtle's art is violent. He is fascinated by meat and offal (like the painter Chaim Soutine); or rather, he is fascinated by the play of light on dead flesh. This violent curiosity is directed back towards his father's cock via the word 'wrinkle', in a set of erotic associations that culminates in a moment when he wants to masturbate in front of a butcher's shop. This set of associations fetishises the penis in classical terms: it seems to conceal an Oedipal drive to make meat of the father's penis, to cut out the law of the father.

Mothers

If, in White's novels, fathers are present mainly in their absence, mothers are almost everywhere. From the beginning White's fictional mothers make unmistakable autobiographical references: in *The Living and the Dead*, White projects his sense of his mother's relation to him into Mrs Standish's ambitions for Elyot: 'She hoped that he would be a writer. If only one of her children were creative, her vanity would flourish like a tree, cover the dead branches of the bitter moments' (*LD* 162). Which means that everything Elyot writes is written, willy-nilly, on behalf of his mother as well. And it is no accident that White's effective career as a novelist ends in *The Twyborn Affair* with a fictional mother, Eadie Twyborn, being reconciled to a wayward son, who is now a woman, Eadith, and who herself/himself repeats, as the names suggest, his mother's self, in however displaced a fashion.

The most remarkable quality of White's mother–son relations is their lack of sexuality and embodiment. Whereas in *The Vivisector* a father's cock can become the piece of meat that erotically charges all flesh, White's most fully described mother, Elizabeth Hunter in *The Eye of the Storm*, is pictured through jewel-imagery. She glitters and changes according to her setting; she seduces; she is flawed; but finally she is asexual, closer to cold death than to the flesh. This is how White describes Mrs Hunter as an old woman in the eye of a hurricane:

> Just as she was no longer a body, least of all a woman: the myth of her womanhood had been exploded by the storm. She was instead a being, or more likely a flaw at the centre of this jewel of light: the jewel itself, blinding and tremulous at the same time, existed, flaw and all, only by grace. (*ES* 409)

It seems as if White negotiated the gap between the mother as origin (the body of which her children have been a part) and mother as individual (an ageing person with all the indignities that ageing imposes on women in our culture) by imagining her as a thing — often, as we have seen, a room or a house, but in this case a jewel.[1] And this remains true even though in White's fictions the mother is characteristically a desiring force, an agent, while the father remains a passive force for stability. To take just one instance, in *The Aunt's Story* it is the mother who wishes to travel and sell off pieces of the family estate, while the father would be happy enough to stay put.

We can say that White tends to reify his fictional mothers' bodies (figure them as things) while his fathers' bodies are fetishised. It would be possible to speculate on the origins of this familial structuration of his fictions, or of his fantasies. But let us instead examine more closely what remains the decisive moment in White's fictional mothers' lives: the moment they die.

White's imagination belongs to a history here too: the death of the mother has been one of the commonest *topoi* of the novel, beginning with what is sometimes called the first modern novel of them all, the Contesse de La Fayette's *La Princesse de Clèves*. In an eighteenth-century novel such as Jean Jacques Rousseau's *La Nouvelle Héloïse*, the mother's death marks the possibility of a child's freedom: Julie's mother's death sanctifies the virtuous mother's memory (it makes her virtue an ideal rather than a living fact) and sets Julie free to become a desiring agent. In the modernist male novel, however, the screw is twisted further: the novelist/hero may often feel responsibility and guilt at his mother's death (as in Lawrence and Joyce) because the advantages of her absence are so clear. She prevents the novelist/hero from being the great experimental artist he is destined to be; she threatens his own claim to masculinity, all the more so because (in White and maybe Proust) both his ambitions for himself and his sexual self-identification are acquired from her.

In White's case, guilt is less apparent. In real life, Ruth's death allowed him to write a different kind of novel: he could come out of the closet, at least partly, to produce what he himself recognised as his best work, *The Solid Mandala*, in which his cosmic claims are set aside, never wholly to return. After his mother's death he becomes a more secular, maybe even a more modest, writer. His fictions, though, tell rather different stories: a mother's death often permits a productive fragmentation of self. Characteristically, *The Aunt's Story* opens with just such a death, narrated laconically and in anonymous relief, 'But old Mrs Goodman did die at last', and that death sets Mrs Goodman's daughter Theodora free to begin her journey to madness.

More generally, a mother's death allows the self to be taken over (or rather, inhabited) by other voices, other identities. This may be true even of characters whose mothers only appear in a sentence or two. Take Laura Trevelyan of *Voss*: here, at the novel's beginning, she is staying at home while others are at church:

> Already she herself was threatening to disintegrate into the voices of the past. The rather thin, grey voice of the mother, to which she had never succeeded in attaching a body. She is going, they said, the kind voices that close the lid and arrange the future. Going, but where? It was cold upon the stairs, going down, down, and glittering with beeswax, until the door opened on the morning, and steps that Kate had scoured with holystone. Poor, poor little girl. She warmed at pity, and on other voices, other kisses, some of the latter of the moist kind. Often the Captain would lock her in his greatcoat, so that she was almost part of him — was it his heart or his supper? — as he gave orders and told tales by turns; all smelled of salt and

men. The little girl was falling in love with an immensity of stars, or the warmth of his rough coat, or sleep. (*Voss* 12)

The first voice of the past that opens up in her tells her of her mother's death ('She is going') and then other voices narrated in the indirect free style pour through her to fill the absence left by her mother's loss. Julie-like, these other voices are more than voices. Locked in the Captain's greatcoat, the little girl becomes 'almost a part' of him, in a flashback heavy with sexual overtones. She asks herself whether this was part of 'his heart or his supper' but, as the Captain smells of 'salt and men', the implication is that it is a more private part still. So it is not just that Laura 'disintegrates' and ceases to be an ordinary self-contained young woman because she is possessed by other voices and other loves (even a love for 'an immensity of stars'). She becomes, specifically, part man, and not just any part. She is phallicised. This is the precondition both for her later obsession with Voss and for her capacity to communicate with him mystically, to internalise his voice from afar. Laura's character, which is not really her own character at all, is formed around the loss of her mother.

Why is a mother's death so enabling in White? As we have begun to see, there are as many reasons as there are registers or ways of thought for providing a reason — psychological, sociological, autobiographical and so on. But the important point is that a mother's death is pivotal in White because for him (as for other modernist writers) a mother is always already near death: she is empty inside. A kind of narcissism is at work here. The logic behind this hidden reasoning is: my mother is a thing because I am no longer in and of her. All that was living in her is now in me.

To imagine the mother as empty is also to imagine her as driven by a desire that is only to be expressed by demands for love. These may become rapacious, as when Mrs Hunter of *The Eye of the Storm*, having committed adultery with her solicitor, instructs the solicitor's wife — her social inferior — to 'Love me!', in another utterly unsuitable demand for love (*ES* 518). What, we might ask, is the relation between Mrs Hunter as jewel, as thing and as desiring force? She desires so much because what she finally desires is to be fully human, to have a full, autonomous subject position, to be able, for instance, to narrate her own novel, instead of having to have a son to do it — which, of course, threatens the writer-son.

Wrong sex

Because maternal presence is so powerful, many of White's fictional children never quite leave the family. Siblings repeatedly have sex with each other: the Brown brothers, Basil and Dorothy Hunter; even Hurtle and his stepsister Rhoda end up living together, though in that case sex is out of the question. As Dorothy Hunter says to her brother Basil, 'What have we got unless each other? Aren't we — otherwise — bankrupt?' (*ES* 508). Families in White's novels implode because children do not possess enough sexual desire or sexual imagination to reach out and attach themselves permanently to partners outside the family, all the more so because their parents' economic power presses on them so heavily. Sex as an element in loving and communicating with another person — humanist sex, we could call it — becomes difficult, almost impossible.

This is not simply a failure. Let us not forget that White was profoundly disenchanted by a society in which 'love' and marriage go together like a horse and carriage, and by a social order based on compulsorily heterosexual marriage as the seal of familial life. White's incestuous relationships — that between Arthur and Waldo Brown, for example — are affirmed, with qualifications, because they stand outside all this: they may reveal a failure of energy and imagination, a regression to the false safety of childhood nostalgia, but they also demonstrate a certain angry, non-conformist will, and a pragmatic capacity to take comfort where it can found.

For White, incest has a great deal in common with same-sex sex. Like incest, homosexuality was prohibited, closeted, for most of his lifetime. To be a homosexual was to be heterodox, and therefore especially able to identify with other marginal or excluded groups. 'As a homosexual I have always known what it is to be an outsider. It has given me added insight into the plight of the immigrant — the hate and contempt with which he is often received,' he once remarked (*Life* 248). But homosexuality reaches much more deeply into White's fictions than incest, partly because he was himself gay (he recognised his own sexuality when young: 'I was chosen as it were, and soon accepted the fact of my homosexuality') but also because homosexuality, in its exchanges with other social forms, has been crucial to modern culture, particularly art-culture (*FG* 35). To understand male homosexuality in White we need some grasp of modern homosexuality's wider history.

As recent historians have made clear, 'homosexuality' as a concept and social category was invented in the late nineteenth century, when a particular form of sexual activity (sex between men) was placed under the management of doctors and police.[2] A homosexual came to be identified by the object of his desires rather than by his acts or desires themselves. Furthermore, a homosexual's object-choice was deemed to be constitutive of his whole personality, and could only be explained by inquiries into the depths of the personality (for psychoanalysis, into the vicissitudes of childhood Oedipal relations).

This psycho-medical idea of homosexuality was intertwined with, and sometimes competed with, an older one in which sex between men was conceived of as inverted heterosexuality. 'Passive' homosexuals were to 'active' homosexuals as women were to men. All this has a larger historical context: during the nineteenth century it became increasingly difficult officially to imagine a good life outside the affectionate heterosexual family, but at the same time forms of relatively classless and exclusively masculine sociability — in the workplace, on the sports field and so on — also became increasingly widely valued. The invention of 'homosexuality' in effect preserved the difference between domestic heterosexuality and public homosociality and maintained their autonomy by closing down on exchanges between the two spheres.

Under this system, often called the regime of compulsory heterosexuality, homosexuals lived in the closet. This is a little simple. The closet too has its history and geography; it was roomier and more open in some times and places than in others. Certainly (returning now to White and his novels) during the 1930s and 1940s homosexuality was much more acceptable and able to be lived openly in London theatre circles than, for instance, in a Sydney suburb. During the 1970s, however, this began to change, as the gay movement began to make it possible for people to live their homosexuality publicly. White himself remained suspicious of the gay liberation movement, as it was then known, even if he came out in *The Twyborn Affair* and *Flaws in the Glass*. He was suspicious partly because gay pride seemed actually to increase the importance of sexuality to personality and life as a whole, partly because he had internalised his own homosexuality both as a 'disease' and as feminising, and partly too because it was easy to exaggerate the fear surrounding the closet and the silence it imposed, especially in White's case. At any rate, for many years one need not have read too deeply between the lines of his publicity to recognise that his sexual partnership was with another man, and his novels consistently, if often obliquely, thematise sex between men. Indeed, being in the closet was productive for White's novelistic techniques.

It may be that the gay movement was less important to White in its politics than its repositioning of the homosexual body. Under the regime of compulsory heterosexuality, the stereotypical closeted homosexual was linked to femininity, as much a woman as a real man. When gay men began working to normalise their sexuality, they did so at first by masculinising it. In the 1970s, moustaches, jeans, cowboy belts and so on — icons of conventional hyper-masculinity — became very popular among gay men, as did (slightly later) hard, pumped bodies. But White had internalised an older manner of homosexuality, although he had never acted out the queeny role (or realised, either in life or in fiction, the deconstructive potential of 'camp' parodic mimicry). In fact he would appear to have eroticised old, flabby flesh: grey bellies that look like they were 'made out of witchetty grubs', as Alf Dubbo memorably puts it in *Riders in the Chariot* (330). In *The Twyborn Affair*, when he deals full-on with a successful gay relationship, he chooses a relationship between a young cross-dresser and an old man (imagining himself as both characters).

This takes us back to White's representations of fathers: at least in his writing, his sexualisation of scraggly, dirtyish, dripping old bodies is a residue of memories of an older man's (especially a father's) body becoming suddenly sexualised for a child. Nance's memory (in *The Vivisector*) of being fucked by her father as a little girl, feeling revulsion but then longing for it to happen again, is perhaps the most graphic instance. There seems little doubt that there is a personal trace here: in his autobiography White recalls a moment when, as a small boy, his headmaster embraced him, holding him against his stomach instead of caning him; he also remembers the complicity between his father and himself over his first erection. One logic of this sexual-object choice is clear: when he becomes the sexual object of older men, White puts himself (or is put) in his mother's place, and he takes that place as much in disgust as in pleasure. But there is a political aspect to this too: old men's flesh, disgusting and desirable all at once, embodies for White a collapse of authoritative masculinity. It is as if these men in power (fathers, headmasters) are also mounds of flesh, and his simultaneous, contradictory desires for and against authority can be brought together as he fetishises their (flabbier as well as stiffer) body parts. And this complex, politicised fetishisation is something that the gay liberation movement, in its early days, made harder.

The beauty of the closet

White's homosexuality interacts with his writing most powerfully not because, as he (falsely) believed, it enabled him to construct better women characters, or even because he used his writing to express transgressive, anti-parental drives, but because it put him in the closet. As he himself knew, without the closet he would not have been the writer that he was. Especially early on, the closet worked in quite conventional ways to shape his writing: it meant, for instance, that he transformed real-life same-sex relationships into fictional opposite-sex ones. Yet even such conventional resignification intensified both his life and work. For instance, in *The Living and the Dead*, he turned his encounter with the American jazz pianist Sam Walsh into a humiliating affair between saxophonist Wally Collins and his hero's mother, Mrs Standish (*Life* 176). With wonderful economy, this allowed him both to stage his belief that he was living out his mother's life, and to humiliate his mother, because she would read the book.

The closet offers more than the possibility of that kind of move. Like the family house, it is both damaging and enabling: better still, it is enabling *because* it is damaging. One of White's clearest articulations of this logic comes quite early in his career in *Riders in the Chariot*, when the young Alf Dubbo is seduced by his protector, the Reverend Timothy Calderon, and they are caught having sex by Calderon's nasty sister, Mrs Pask. When Calderon tries to confess and take the blame, she responds 'I do not know, Timothy, what you are referring to' (*RC* 333). It becomes clear that this flat disavowal is not just a means of maintaining appearances (that is, the closet); it is a way by which Mrs Pask can establish control over Timothy, a form of blackmail. So in fact it is the poor young Aboriginal artist, Dubbo, who profits from the situation: his paintings, which Mrs Pask regards as 'horrible, horrible obscenities' (334), gain their aura, their power to evoke otherness, from his closeted sexual experiences. In this way they also allegorise the novel itself, written as it is by a (half) closeted homosexual.

In fact the closet is important to White because its structure, in which the private (and, often, what is especially valuable in life) is figured as what is withdrawn from public gaze, covers so much more than homosexuality. But modern subjectivity in general has the structure of an open secret in the sense that individual lives are shaped by institutions and values that must be retreated from, but not radically broken from, in order for full interiority to be achieved. White himself acted this structure out in his life in an almost emblematic form, intensified as it was by his sexuality. Early on in his autobiography he tells a moving anecdote in which, as a little boy, he led the clergyman he had a crush on (shades of Alf Dubbo) into a cave to share secrets hidden in a cardboard box (*FG* 72). Such half-secret receptacles, as we know, will become common in his novels: often, like the box in *The Living and the Dead*, gifts that conceal as much as they reveal of the giver.

The closet is not just a social structure: it is also a spiritual and aesthetic/textual one. At the spiritual level, there is what we might call an ontology of the closet to which White was deeply attached. His religious experiences and his novel-writing were repeatedly articulated as a revelation of the world's deepest, most all-encompassing secrets, an unveiling of dangerous truths (*Life* 284). It follows that there is an aesthetics of the closet: symbolism itself. As we have already seen, White thought of his works as hiding their true and 'profoundest' meanings. To give just one instance of the ease with which he conceived of his novels in this way: after receiving encouragement from Huebsch over *The Tree of Man*, White wrote to him: 'I don't know whether other authors experience what I do: a feeling that they may be writing a secret language that nobody else will be able to interpret. Consequently the strain is very great until one discovers it is intelligible to someone else. And this time the strain has been increasing over four years' (*Life* 299). As the most influential modernist aestheticians have insisted, in our period art becomes 'art' only in works whose meaning is 'veiled', as Theodor Adorno, borrowing from Walter Benjamin, put it.[3]

It is not as though the meanings that the work veils actually exist. Eve Sedgwick theorises the closet as modernist writing's 'empty secret' — its evacuation of representational content, which according to her is connected to a cultural disavowal of the desired male body.[4] It makes more sense to me to think about modernist writing's concealment of its meaning as directed towards a highly specialised and professionalised reading community willing to labour over these works as if that labour might indeed reveal something of substance and value. Still the modernist work, like the closeted homosexual, each with their half-open secrets, proliferates ambiguity and interpretation that, in both cases, breed desire. Is he or isn't he? Is that brush against a leg just accidental? What is the meaning of Arthur's mandala in *The Solid Mandala*? These questions share the closet's hermeneutics: what is sometimes called 'paranoid knowing' — 'it takes one to know one' — either a homosexual or a modernist. In a society where sexual preferences are out, openly declared, or at least in which they *ought* to be out, such questions and the anticipations of pleasure that produce them (and are intensified by them) become less common and less valued. Then we are in postmodern as against modern culture. White, at least until his late postmodern turn, writing from the closet, called upon the closet's capacity to generate desire in order to construct his preternaturally sensitive and self-aware characters and his 'profound' fictions. But he remains constrained by the limits of this structure: in him too ambiguous desire can only last so long; once it has been fulfilled the closet has been opened, its emptiness revealed and its intensities dissipated.

This hermeneutics of the closet operates most powerfully in *Voss* and the male community of the expedition it describes — a community that, as it travels towards disaster, nurtures a number of open and half-open homosexual loves, jealousies, interdependencies and obsessions. There is a sense in which Voss's journey is an excuse for White to imagine a highly sexualised community without women, and the expedition's tragic end can be read as an expression of his internalisation of homophobia as guilt. Yet this community also seems like a community of homosexuals travelling, if this were possible, both away from and further into the closet. And it invites its readers into the closet by tempting them simultaneously to hunt out symbols (what does Voss's quest really stand for?) and homosexuality (what kind of desire flows between these men, and between whom?). All this is possible because homosexuality in *Voss* is primary, not a deviant turn from a norm. It is the shape male sexuality takes when men make contact with their primordial, quasi-unconscious nature (which is what their quest into Australia's interior signifies). Homosexuality in *Voss* belongs to the closet, but at the same time it is primordial for men.

Here, close to the novel's beginning, is Frank Le Mesurier, the 'exquisite' immigrant intellectual and poet, reacting to the drunken working-class Turner:

> Anything that was physically repulsive to him, he would have trodden under foot. He would not have cared to brush against Turner, yet it was probable, riding through the long, yellow grass, their stirrup-irons would catch at each other in overtures of intimacy, or lying in the dust and stench of ants, wrestling with similar dreams under the stars, their bodies would roll over and touch. (*Voss* 42)

Characteristically, the concreteness and sensory thickness of Le Mesurier's imaginings (those ants, that grass's yellowness) are the displacement of his unfulfilled and undeclared sexuality: not brushing against Turner becomes lying and wrestling together on the earth.

Le Mesurier's unacted dream of sex with Turner will have important consequences for Voss's troupe. Turner will later fall in love with the young pastoralist, Ralph Angus, and Angus and Turner unite against Voss and Le Mesurier as one jealous couple against another. Ralph Angus and Turner talk about Le Mesurier at a crucial moment:

> 'That is one I cannot cotton to, Ralph.'
> The young landowner winced, and was loath to criticise a man who might possibly be considered a member of his own class.

'He is an odd sort of cove. He is different,' finally he replied.

'Not so different from some,' Turner said.

'What do you imply by that?' asked Angus, who did not care to become involved in any unpleasantness.

He was what you would call a pleasant fellow, no one had anything against him, and now he did a little repent of his rash friendship.

'Eh?' mumbled Turner, resentfully.

'What do you mean, then?'

'Voss is what I mean. And Le Mesurier.'

Angus tingled.

'In this expedition, which is what it is called,' Turner said, or whispered, rather, from habit, 'we are made up of oil and water, you might say, and will not run together, ever.'

. . .

'We understand each other, Ralph, you and me.' (*Voss* 254)

Everything in this passage is determined by the closet, its expressive silences and double-talk.

What is Le Mesurier's 'difference' as these characters see it? On one — the open — level, his artiness, his being an intellectual, a modernist even. But, as Turner says, he is 'not so different from some', which in the code of the closet means not so different from Turner and Angus and their 'unpleasant' love. This is how Angus seems to interpret the remark. It is because Le Mesurier is not so different from Turner and Angus (which the reader already knows, knowing how he desired Turner earlier) that his and Voss's relation may be thought of as not so different either. In fact, if we return to the moment when Voss talks Le Mesurier into accompanying him, it is a kind of seduction, one that leaves Le Mesurier 'throbbing' (35). So Angus and Turner's defection from Voss and Le Mesurier is (among other things) the rejection of one couple by another, in part because Le Mesurier has not been able to enact his desire for Turner. That defection helps seal Voss's fate.

It does so all the more effectively because another couple is forming alongside Voss/Le Mesurier and Angus/Turner. In his 'craving for earthly love', the tough and practical ex-convict Judd forms an alliance with Harry Robarts, a rather slow adolescent.

They were riding and drowsing in perpetual dust . . . when Judd reached over and grabbed something from the trunk of a tree.

'There you are, Harry,' he said, and offered his closed, hairy hand. 'There is a present for yer . . .'

'What is it?' asked the boy, advancing his own hand, but cautiously.

'No,' laughed Judd, blushing under the dirt. 'Open your mouth, shut your eyes.'

Then, when his suggestion had been followed, he popped a little lump of gum into the lad's open mouth.

'Aoh!' cried Harry, wrinkling up.

'No,' insisted Judd. 'Go on.'

He was putting into his own mouth a similar knot of gum, to demonstrate his faith in the token, or else they would both die of it.

So they rode, and sucked the gum, which was almost quite insipid in flavour, if slightly bitter. Yet, they were both to some extent soothed and united by its substance and their act, and were prodding the rumps of the broken cattle with their toes . . . (*Voss* 245)

It is a passage that repeats and anticipates those scenes from White's other novels in which gifts are given: Connie's gift of a glass box to Elyot in *The Living and the Dead*, Arthur Brown's gift of a marble to his brother in *The Solid Mandala*. In this light, the exchange of a box with a magnifying glass becomes not just a love gift but an emblem of a desire for a certain kind of containment, and places these characters against Voss, that man of wide, open landscapes, deserts and sands. But the gift is also a sexual exchange, just like those that *Voss*'s characters are making. Judd's blushing gives the game away, and the sucking of the gum, somewhat oddly called a unifying 'act', leads directly to a kind of miming of a sexual act, when Judd and Harry prod the rumps of their cows. It is also an allegory of the text itself, a gift from White to his readers from the closet that reveals and hides his homosexuality, and promises more meaning, more profundity than it is actually able to communicate.

5 NARRATIVE TECHNIQUES

I have argued that White's life and writing were organised to achieve his recognition as a genius. It was as part of this effort that he developed his fiction's teasing profundity. But he also introduced teasing autobiographical references, most obviously in *The Vivisector*, where the main character, the painter Hurtle Duffield, stands for White himself. '*The Vivisector* is more about myself than any other — my unfortunate character at least — though in very different circumstances,' he wrote (*Life* 476).

The Vivisector celebrates the pathology of genius: as White said of himself, 'my writing seems to be a disease for which there is no cure' (*Life* 349). Hurtle paints so well and has such a meteoric career only by hurting those who want warmth from him. As Nance, the prostitute who loves him, says, 'What your sort don't realise . . . is that other people exist. While you're all gummed up in the great art mystery, they're alive, and breakun their necks for love' (*V* 197). Or, again, as White's one-time friend Klári Daniel said of White himself, 'He squeezes you out like a lemon and when it is dry he turns to someone else' (*Life* 455).

For White, geniuses must be prepared to hurt those close to them because their art requires transgressive, experimental experiences; as Freud put it, their 'cultural work' results from the 'repression' of 'perverse elements'.[1] Genius is destructive because, for the genius, life is finally material to be turned into art-as-truth. Thus those who share a genius's life can never be treated as ends-in-themselves, as independent human beings; they remain secondary to the work they feed. Artists are unable to love, where 'love' stands for the relation that one person has with another when their mutual separateness is reciprocally most felt and respected. White's belief involves at least an apparent self-critique: he does not really know what love is, and this critique is personified in White's characters, as his autobiographical aesthetic demands. He repeatedly shows characters as ambivalent about each other, or, to put it another way, as if the received vocabularies for describing intimate connections between people suppose more constancy and transparency in relationships than he can attest to.

It follows from this autobiographical aesthetic that the critic needs to read White's life alongside his works, and it is worth reminding ourselves that White himself was fascinated by, and drew from, the long biographies of canonical modernist writers that appeared in the 1950s (George Painter on Proust, Leon Edel on Henry James, Richard Ellmann on Joyce). During the war he spent some time writing a (never-performed) dramatisation of Henry James's *The Aspern Papers*, a novella based on Lord Byron's life, which pits the cruel genius both against his loved ones and against a rather creepy scholar sniffing out the genius's letters. It was a telling choice. Critics are all the more dangerous for artists who subscribe to the autobiographical aesthetic of perversity because the critic (like the friend or lover, but unlike the hagiographic biographer) need not accept the geniuses' evaluation of their own 'perversity'.

The notion that authors' lives ground their writing in general is historically specific. It first appears at the end of the nineteenth century, when it became difficult to produce masterpieces either by adhering to traditional literary conventions or by naturalistically mirroring society. A tight connection between personal experience and novel-writing had been unthinkable for earlier novelists — those like Jane Austen, say, who told conventional moral love stories (almost always ending in happy marriages) bearing only the vaguest relation to their own lives. White's grounding of art in personal experience and values also involves a departure from earlier modernist writers such as Henry James and Gertrude Stein, who were primarily interested in formal experimentalism. In fact, many modernist schools made no appeal to artists' lives or to any communicable wisdom based on their genius. Constructivists, for example embraced technology; urban modernists — *flâneurs* — invested the detritus of urban culture with powerful nostalgia (Louis Aragon, Joseph Cornell); the surrealists embraced chance and fate for their project of total estrangement from the ordinary; others flirted with what has been called vulgar modernism, absorbing industrialised popular culture into art-genres (like Nathanael West or John Dos Passos).

In deploying a self-presentational strategy that first appeared in second-generation naturalist writers as different as Frank Norris and James Joyce, White was, once again, a little dated, though by no means unusual. The stronger tradition even within late modernism has been either to move further from realism than Joyce, say, into a form of allegory, as in Beckett; or to figure writing as self-referential play, as in Nabokov. Fully fledged postmodernist writers such as Walter Abish or Thomas Pynchon can no longer accept the whole conceptual structure through which the artist is deemed great by virtue of a private vision expressed in the work.

The writing/life relation has a specific twist in a modernist like White. To put a complicated matter simply: through his fictions, White claimed to tell deeper, less stereotypical truths than those circulated within, for instance, popular media. Where are these profound truths to be found? In his novels' symbolic structures, of course, but also in the manner through which White's own life-experiences are imaginatively transformed and elaborated into art-fictions. White's narrative voice — the narrator who tells the stories — expresses wisdom that the implied reader is asked to believe is White's own. This wisdom, however, rarely takes the form of propositions in the narrative voice deemed to be true both of the real and the fictional world. It is an almost invisible wisdom: the implicit standard that makes the fictions golden; the invisible screen on which they can be projected as profound and vivid.

To take one of thousands of possible examples, in *Riders in the Chariot*, Mrs Godbold's daughter Else falls under the bushes in an erotic tangle with her boyfriend Bob Tanner:

> The present welcomed them with open arms. As they rocked together, underneath the elder bush, it did not seem very likely that anything would ever withstand Bob Tanner's blunt conviction.

'I will show you! I will hold you! I will give you the future!'

'Ah, Bob! Bob!' Else cried.

As if she had not always known that all certainty was here, and goodness must return, like grass. (*RC* 467)

Here Else's knowledge that 'all certainty was here, and goodness must return, like grass' is not knowledge true once and for all. It is true for a fictional character at a certain fictional time and place. Yet it is not quite Else's own knowledge either: its language is more that of the narrator and his supposed reader than Else herself. It possesses overtones of 'wisdom', the wisdom of White's characteristic affirmation of sexual transgression and earthiness, all the more so because, as is so often the case, the dialogue is written in an idiolect that the character would not speak in life. So what is it that serves to ground this passage, to persuade the reader that it works? A faith in what is not actually there in the text but appealed to and claimed: the author's imagination and genius. And, I would argue, this in turn rests on a reader's faith that the author — White — has experienced this kind of thing himself, even if not literally: that these words on the page picture a reality that was not just imagined *ex nihil* in acts of pure creativity, but is true to the tenor of his life-experiences.

White's confessions of his belief that his disease and his genius were twinned were less insights into the roots of literary talent than signs that the way in which he conceived the relation between literature and society was becoming difficult, indeed impossible. White's strategies for figuring himself as a writer, and the writing practices that followed, were extraordinarily effective; he was successful in establishing himself as Australia's pre-eminent novelist. What then of the genius as cruel, lost outsider? In his success, White's linking his genius to his pathologies begins to seem complacent and self-serving in ways it was not for earlier writers who never gained recognition during their lifetime. And once we give up on the theory that talented writers have particularly profound insights into existence based on their marginal and hence special personal experience, and their capacity to sacrifice life for writing, then the whole genre of art-novel to which White was dedicated becomes impossible to write — which is more or less what has happened.

One problem with the idea that White deployed his life to become a great national novelist is that it does not account for his novels' structures. Even under an aesthetic where novels are supposed to express the truth of life, life is different from novels, not just because life is real while novels are fictional, but because novels are highly and artificially organised, whereas lives are not, or less so. A novel is a completed whole made up of elements whose assemblage involves innumerable choices. Novelists must ask themselves such questions as: how many characters should I use? should one character be central? should I use first-person or third-person narration? divide the book into chapters? narrate this event from this or that character's point of view? begin this chapter like this or like that? and so on. In life there are fewer such choices.

Let us take *The Vivisector* as an example of this difference between life-structure and fiction-structure, because it is expressed as an almost hidden gap between Hurtle's fictional life and his aesthetic values that are supposed to hold good outside the fiction. As we have seen, like White, Hurtle paints out of himself and his experiences; he is driven by a need to express his vision in colour and paint at the cost of love. Yet, while the notion of a driven, self-consuming genius does transfer into White's own idea of himself, *The Vivisector* is not itself simply guided by an autobiographical aesthetic. The distance between the novel's narrative voice and implied author on the one hand and Hurtle on the other is crucial to this difference: the novel knows more about Hurtle than he does about himself, and it articulates this knowledge through its chosen structure. We can put it like this: Hurtle is an instinctive artist, but the novel can present his character because it is not simply instinctive itself. As so often, this gap becomes most apparent as the novel ends. When Hurtle is dying, the text characteristically lapses into a fragmented, barely meaningful stream of consciousness, apparently losing its coherence. Hurtle, barely conscious, becomes obsessed with the word 'INDIGO', and dies punning on it: 'indiggodd' — a twist by which this painter-colourist gets into his own kind of heaven after death: the heaven (in god) of the colour indigo. The point is that this twist is highly contrived (too highly contrived, in my opinion). At the moment when the character's consciousness becomes unthreaded, and the narrative seems to lose coherence, structure and authorial cleverness are in fact dominant. All the more so because a well-trained reader will now scurry back into the novel, tracing the use of colour-names across earlier pages in order to let their differences and repetitions saturate the text with as much meaning as possible. This kind of interpretation and the structuration it depends on are important to White, but not to Hurtle. In fact, White is caught between two aesthetics — or more accurately, between an aesthetic and a technique. Like Hurtle, he wishes to claim genius by expressing his life-experiences truthfully and immediately in his novels in an aesthetic grounded on his exceptionalism and pain, but he is also necessarily driven to deal with technical questions of organising his text to maximise the amount of meaning and profundity it can communicate. As we will see, his techniques sometimes fail him, and they do so, I would argue, because he remained so committed to an autobiographical aesthetic of perverse genius.

Writing practices

What, then, were White's writing techniques? They began in the writing situation itself. Though he wrote 'out of himself', his status as a 'great' writer, the bearer of his culture's profoundest values, began to affect his writing in a feedback mechanism. We know that his work, which quarries his everyday wisdom and experience, is also work *on* his life, in the sense that he lived to write. This meant that he needed to live a life that could offer him material, but was also ascetic enough to produce highly individuated texts. Personal discipline mediates between the autobiographical expressiveness and the structure of his fictions. So too does the way that White believed he became his characters, in a merger of self and fictional characters which is in turn thematised. Theodora at the end of *The Aunt's Story*, for instance, is no longer able to distinguish experiences happening to her from experiences happening to characters she imagines. Her madness is an undisciplined unravelling of the productive disease of the great fiction writer.

What forms of control or discipline did White possess? For him, writing was half violent struggle, half spiritual exercise — rather as late modernists like Georges Bataille thought of it in the 1930s. This is White on the hard graft of writing in his autobiography:

> What do I believe? I am accused of not making it explicit. How to be explicit about a grandeur too overwhelming to express, a daily wrestling match with an opponent whose limbs never become material, a struggle from which the sweat and blood are scattered on the pages of anything the serious writer writes? A belief contained less in what is said than in the silences. (*FG* 70)

This echoes White's descriptions of Hurtle painting in *The Vivisector* (which seem to be partly based, in turn, on Virginia Woolf's descriptions of Lily Bristow in *To the Lighthouse*, as well as on the publicity surrounding 'action painters' such as Jackson Pollock). It is a curiously physical and bloody description of the scene of writing. On the other side, White's writing had a ritualistic, almost obsessional aspect: he wrote and rewrote his drafts (one, two, three) in a certain progressive pattern. For him writing was also 'art' in the sense that it could gain energy by conversion from other artistic forms. As we know, White's movement into literary modernism was made via painting. But music was at least as important to his writing. He wrote to or around music to help him capture a mood: Mahler and Alban Berg for *Voss*; Bloch's second sonata for violin for *Riders in the Chariot* (music that enabled him, he said, with the hubris of self-ascribed genius, 'to know inside me what it means to be a Jew'), Stockhausen for the night that Hurtle visits his retrospective, and so on. The act of writing, then, was as much a discipline that leads to grace (to use a classic Catholic formulation) as a violent ordeal. Privacy was very important to him; his partner Lascaris read the novels only at the third-draft stage. The rigid and solitary performance of writing permitted White to alter consciousness and identity as he wrote: alone in his discipline and violence, he became his characters, or rather, shaman-like, his characters revealed themselves inside him so that he could write them down.

It is tempting to consider White's writing technique and his creation of characters as connected in a particular way, as if the ascetic, ritualistic situation of writing enabled the trance out of which creative energy poured, focused on character production. The trouble is that many of White's characters are stereotypes: they are cut and pasted from widely disseminated discursive resources. What we can say, though, is that White once more displaced the conditions of writing as he represented them to himself onto some of his novels and characters: the solitude, aestheticism and repetitions that enabled him to write are shared by certain of his characters, or at least there is a sense that, when they try to free themselves from such conditions, they achieve freedom only at the price of reason. The characters that carry most ethical and emotional intensity seem to live their lives in conditions that partly mimic those through which White himself could be a writer, even if, unlike their author, they often fail: Voss, Theodora, Waldo of *The Solid Mandala* and then, successfully, Hurtle.

Diegesis

We can now move from the scene of White's writing to the structure of the writing itself. I want to concentrate on three elements: plot, character and closure. In White's novels, plot (or diegesis) is not as important as it was in nineteenth-century realism, where it provided the means by which characters as private selves could be located within, and reconciled to, society, enabling the text to tell a story that encapsulated history as progress. In the classic realist novel, endings in which selves became morally transparent (virtue being rewarded, vice punished) pointed towards a more ordered society. In White, however, as in other modernists, characters' subjectivities burst out of the plot, which becomes a scaffolding for the presentation of private consciousnesses.

What happens in the typical White novel? Plot in the sense of suspense, mystery, adventure barely exists (with the possible exceptions of *Voss* and *A Fringe of Leaves*). Leaving aside 'sensational' uses of plot, there is not even much experimentation with story time: White's only real play with temporality is in the use of flashbacks to achieve effects of wholeness. More importantly, characters do not interact with a strongly plotted flow of incident. As monadic selves, characters grow, love, hate, talk, travel, test themselves and break down against a minimally sketched social or historical background. Occasionally they experience or enact an external crisis or irruption — fire, flood, war — but these cataclysms rarely if ever transform them. If they did, then the texts would be based on the kind of interaction between character and external event constitutive of nineteenth-century plots. Even historical crises like the Second World War come from nowhere; structurally they are no different from natural disasters such as floods. All these things mean that White's plots tend to be paratactic or serial: one thing happens, then another, then another, and events — a death, a birth, a house-sale, whatever — only refer to or implicate each other through the main characters' usually rather passive and self-absorbed emotional or spiritual responses to them. This means that characters' personalities are given; they do not change as the plot progresses. At best, they gradually reveal their real selves in unexpected ways (like Waldo Brown or Hurtle Duffield).

So plot does not provide White's novels with their structure, or what critics used to call their 'form'. This does not mean that he deploys the structural principle developed by early modernist writers, especially Henry James, through which plot was replaced by point of view as an organising principle. That is, White's novels are not structured within a carefully constructed framework by first presenting an event from one character's point of view and then from another character's point of view and so on, even though White does describe most events through a character's consciousness. He creates structure by using many techniques all together in an ad hoc fashion.

To take some examples: structure is achieved by creating patterns of imagery, especially by associating particular characters with particular objects (Mrs Hunter with mirrors and jewels, for instance), or by repetitions in which what one character does in one context another does in another context (Elyot refusing sex while listening to music and then his sister Eden having sex thrust upon her while also listening to music, in *The Living and the Dead*), or by making the end of the novel refer back to the beginning, or by creating narrative rhythms in which minor characters chorally comment on the action.

White's refusal of plot is in fact allegorised in his texts through his use of those apparently trivial but durable objects that are mentioned repeatedly across various scenes as the object of a character's attention or even love or obsession: the marbles that Arthur Brown hoards for himself in *The Solid Mandala*, the glass box that Elyot mysteriously receives in *The Living and the Dead*, General Sokolnikov's nautilus in *The Aunt's Story*. Because of their second-level textual function (they both comment on the text and belong to it), they are worth thinking about at some length. We know that these objects' lack of use value, their enigmatic blankness, seems to promise a meaning for the reader as much as for the characters, a meaning that is not itself part of the plot. We can now add that these strange little objects come also to function as signifiers of a text that is itself in narrative terms undynamic, self-contained.

We can take this further: these objects also signify the opposite of a mode of being in the world about which White is extremely and endlessly ambivalent: the drive to lead a plotted or *committed* life in the existentialist sense rather than the artist's life of retreat. That is, they invite inspection on two levels: in the way that they promise textual meaning independent of plot (and character interaction with plot) and in the way that they signal an aestheticist ethic based on not acting in the world. To take just one instance, in *The Aunt's Story*, the General who (apparently) owns the nautilus shell is also a story-telling bore, though he admires the simplicity of stories that, as he says in a semi-pun, 'put things in a nutshell' (*AS* 216). Such stories, as the reader knows, and as a character reminds us, are 'lies' — which means that the General is also a fictionalist, an artist — so much so, surprisingly, that he does not even create art: his conversation and life are spontaneously fictional, resolutely uncommitted. But in the plot his nautilus shell is acquired by a Mrs Rapello, one of White's mother-figures, *nouveau riche*, pushy; like Mrs Hunter, an ex-beauty and the mother of a princess. The General wants the shell back, and eggs Theodora on to steal it from Mrs Rapello, which she does. Finally, Mrs Rapello and the General fight over and destroy it.

Here an important set of interconnections is set in place across different levels and constituents of the text and its reading situation:

(i) a fictional character, the General, parodic figure of the uncommitted artist and his enigmatic and loved lost possession, symbol of his fictions, the nautilus shell;

(ii)   the shell's heterodiegetic and teasing offer to tell a story and offer a meaning over and above mere plot, a value equivalent to the desire it excites;

(iii)   the General's interminable and tiresome yarns, which are not wholly separate from, or are interpretable as equivalent to, both the shell and the stories that make up *The Aunt's Story* itself;

(iv)   (moving from the diegesis to the implied reader) the reader's assumed need to make full sense of what is being read;

(v)   the 'lies' or fictionality of fiction itself, signalled by the nautilus shell's lack of any true meaning at all, so that its destruction does not really matter; it has no use except as an object of fascination.

By listing these constituents of the text we can see how much this little object, the nautilus shell, sets into play, and how it finally undoes these textual elements and their meaningful connection with another: what is left of all that the shell promises and signifies is nothing, mere splinters on the floor.

So White uses small objects, obsessively possessed by certain characters, both to secure and to critique the value and coherence of his texts. But he also inserts them into the text by contrasting them with other kinds of events, states or objects. Little hard objects are contrasted to destructive or formless ones: floods, fires, the sea and, in *Voss* especially, sand and the desert. In *Voss*, for instance, Laura tells Voss she would rather marry 'sand' than 'stone' (*Voss* 67–8) though, in Voss's absence, she can imagine perfection and stability in stones (122) and Voss is himself (in a Christianising reference) a 'rock' as he travels through the desert (136), though he, in turn, identifies Laura and her relationship with him as a 'desert' (192). The opposition between things (here between sand and stone) once again promises meaning: it is another lure for readers (and most of all critics).

Certainly in *Voss* a set of associations is organised by the opposition between rock and sand. The desert and stone become 'symbols' just by being mentioned so often, and the sheer abstraction of the contrast between sand and stone enables their associations to multiply. Thus the desert, and Voss's will to penetrate it, represents his (desire for) freedom in contrast to seaboard, domestic (heterosexual), ordinary life ("It is not for me, unfortunately so, to build a solid house and live in it the kind of life that is lived in such houses" (131)). The desert represents the mapless grandeur of the universe in relation to Voss's heroic and impossible will to mastery, his urge to wrestle order from existence; it represents death and death's glamour against the superficialities of survival and life. In these terms the novel can be read as a long poem in prose praising the desert and the impossible compulsion to tame it; an elegy, that is, to Voss. The opposition between sand (formless) and stone (form) is plotted: it becomes Voss's quest. In this way the plot is pushed forward, not for its suspense or mystery, but as a means of negotiating the signification of 'symbols'.

Yet White's technique of driving plot forward symbolically, in terms of two sets of contrasting states or kinds of things, remains at odds with his realist tendencies. The relations between his symbols are just too abstract to organise the messy world that he must also treat, committed as he is by his autobiographical aesthetic to represent the nitty-gritty details, the thick experiences of social and psychological life. Ask even the easiest questions that the opposition in *Voss* sets in play: is Laura associated more with rock or with sand? is Voss? Such questions are impossible to answer. This time it is not that the text's 'symbols' point to the impossibility of interpreting them, nor that they turn into conventional signs, but that the textual level at which they work does not connect firmly enough to the realist milieu in which the characters move, and to which their interiority is constantly attuned. And I would argue that, in the last instance, characterisation and the representation of subjectivity is where the novels' real energy and project lies. But I would make a further point: White is driven all the more powerfully towards a socially oriented and autobiographical aesthetic because his texts fail to communicate clear messages. What makes his works more than a collection of nautilus shells like the General's is, more than anything, their relation to his own life and the bunch of characters inhabiting his body.

Characters

As we have seen, for White the private self — the interiority — was like the hoarding of a secret, a (failed) escape from the public gaze. Furthermore, he believed he had a desire to destroy subjectivity as content. In a letter to Geoffrey Dutton he approvingly cites 'a remark by Lieselotte, a character, figment or facet of myself in *The Aunt's Story*: "We must destroy everything, everything, even ourselves. Then at last when there is nothing, perhaps we shall live"' (*Letters*, 539). In effect, White had two finally irreconcilable models for thinking about interiority. On the one hand, subjectivity consists of a series of character routines playing out multiple interior selves. This is true not just for public speech and acts but also for interior and private ones: thoughts, even passions. These private performances are produced, as it were, for the individuals themselves who are thus doubled — simultaneously actor and spectator. On the other hand, subjectivity could possess quite a different shape: it could consist of intensities, memories and eddies of feeling which, in theory, lie outside self-reflection. Thus the empty interior retreat is always threatened by surprises, which may intrude even from within:

> One thinks to escape, but doesn't, or not wholly: the fingerprints were taken early on. The past recurs in the dressing-table mirror, wisps of it in benign dreams, or those darker ones in which unfulfilled, half-forgotten lusts explode. Worst of all are the consciously created fictions, because concrete evidence of what one has not dared admit. (*FG* 46)

So these surprises can come in the form of ghostly selves, interior fictional or dramatic personalities. The two sides of subjective life — either desirable and inaccessible emptiness or internal stage upon which many selves, of either gender, take their turn to perform — are related by a logic expressed early on in Elyot Standish: 'Alone he was not yet alone, imitating as he did the themes of so many other lives' (*LD* 18). To exist as a multiplicity of performed selves is not to have a self of one's own.

Yet in White's descriptions of his characters' deep subjectivity, the theatrical, 'many in one' model often intrudes on the model of empty subjectivity to produce awkwardness and self-consciousness to which White's readers must soon accustom themselves. Let us take an instance from *The Living and the Dead*, a text in which the two conceptions of subjectivity are less effectively reconciled than they will be later. The schoolboy Elyot is meditating:

Going for walks there are always the flat stretches between the corners and the hills, they are pretty well endless, they are like the weeks between events, the cloudy, anonymous weeks that connect phases. Nothing is done that is not tentative, depending on the wind for its direction. In the evening you hang over the gate. You listen to the voices in the lane . . . You get left outside the body of events, like the stone on the antipodal cherry. And not everyone is a Mr Macarthy, sometimes this exasperates, even without knowing why, there is not the substitute of nets. (*LD* 108)

This is half Joycean stream of consciousness — subjectivity as sheer flow — and half self-reflection — consciousness as self-commentary. The passage's implausibility as a representation of even an extremely self-conscious adolescent is signalled and made concrete in White's use of the second-person pronoun ('you') through which Elyot addresses himself. That 'you' makes two Elyots: the Elyot who lives and acts and feels in the world, and the interior Elyot who thinks and watches that worldly Elyot. This second Elyot exists as what linguists sometimes call the 'subject of enunciation', as a function of language, in this case the hidden 'I' who addresses his own (other) self as 'you'. The emptiness of this interior Elyot, his existing as not much more than that hidden 'I', hollows out the character and, more generally, evokes the 'deeper', private self as a stage on which unreal selves perform.

One reason why this technique (which White was never to jettison) does not work is that this 'you' unavoidably also addresses the text's readers. The pronoun of address ('you') puts the reader in the same linguistic position as the character, and thereby achieves a linguistic intimacy between narrator, character and reader; but, because the intimacy is mainly (only?) linguistic, it rings false.

Where White does not use the second-person pronoun he often presents his characters' interiority through 'free indirect discourse', that is, he describes subjectivity from a character's perspective but not in their words. Take this example from *A Fringe of Leaves*, when Ellen is having sex with Garnet Roxburgh:

She was again this great green, only partially desirable, obscene bird, on whose breast he was feeding, gross hands parting the sweeping folds of her tormented and tormenting plumage; until in opening and closing, she might

have been rather, the green, fathomless sea, tossing, threatening to swallow
down the humanly manned ship which had ventured on her. (*FL* 116)

Using a technique perfected by Virginia Woolf, White, in a single sentence, shifts point of view from Garnet to Ellen, that is, from the bird
Ellen is for Garnet to the 'gross hands' Garnet is for Ellen. Or so I read
it. The difficulty is not just sorting out whose consciousness is being
represented here at any particular moment (is she, later in the sentence, a 'green, fathomless sea' for herself or for him?); it is, once more,
that the highly figurative language belongs to the narrator, not to the
characters. They would never use this kind of language themselves;
their emptiness is being filled by the narrator's poetry. In effect, White
here has given up on character construction, letting a writerly discourse take over. Here White's writing, in its sheer literariness, suggests
his own 'greatness' too immediately. Where his characters' interiority
disappears into this kind of prose, as it often does, White has failed to
imagine otherness and to create fictional characters who are more than
narcissistic — which was Hurtle's failure, according to Nance.

This should remind us that White did attempt to puncture his
own narcissism by producing grotesque, parodic self-portraits — most
successfully with Waldo in *The Solid Mandala*. But, at the level of the
sentence, he also used techniques borrowed from surrealism to avoid
using self-regarding imagery. In *The Living and the Dead*, the young
Kitty Goose is being courted by Willy Standish, a feckless would-be
artist, soon to become her husband. While they are drinking, 'He
began to talk about India. It unfolded like a cloud, drenched with
many colours, the forms that intermingled in the formless cloud of
narrative' (*LD* 62). This sentence represents Kitty's drunken consciousness indirectly from her point of view, but the imagery belongs
less to the conventional literariness of the *Fringe of Leaves* passage than
to surrealism. As India becomes a multicoloured cloud melting into
the shapeless cloud of Willy's speech, the language gains power
through the 'juxtaposition of two or more or less distant realities' as
André Breton put it in his first 'Manifesto of Surrealism'.[2] And because
the passage's 'surrealism' does not fit conventional canons of good
taste, it lacks the self-regarding force of much of White's discourses of
interiority.

White often turns to surrealist writing practices to describe moments when his characters are cut loose from social conventions and responsibilities. Often these moments of demoralisation, ageing or drunkenness allow the body violently to upset the social personality, as at the end of *The Living and the Dead* when Mrs Standish hallucinates and shits drunkenly at a party:

> As the legs waved against the wall, all legs, and hair, suspended in the sea, the silence, which was breath held, over this the gurgle in a pewter pint, was Number One, and Number Two, it was tense waiting for the last sigh, that fell back with a last trickle into the empty pot. (*LD* 322)

Here the weird juxtaposition (walls as legs), with its shocks, is designed not to present an empty subjective state but a body pushing consciousness out of coherence. For White such moments are not trivial or pathological. On the contrary they are climactic; they provide turning points or closures. They hint that life cannot be boxed in by literature; that literature fails when it is too coherent or tasteful. Yet the characters whose consciousness surrealism describes are always fictionally contained — here, not least, by the sentence's wonderfully breathy syntax. None the less, in this case, the relation between the syntactical complexity and surrealist vulgarity returns us to 'great writing' as a mode, in a way that surrealism's own emphasis on automatic writing disallowed.

Character construction is not just a matter of interiority. At one level, thinking about characters from the outside, we can ask: what do White's characters look like? Though most are not described in any real visual detail, it seems that for White himself they could be pictured quite minutely, as if playing in a theatre. For instance, when discussing who should play the part of Voss in a projected film version of the novel, he rejected the idea of Donald Sutherland because 'Before all else, that flabby wet mouth is entirely wrong. Voss was dry and ascetic — he had a thin mouth like a piece of fence-wire,' adding that he thought 'a whole characterisation can go astray on a single physical feature like that' (*Letters* 442). Note, however, that here Voss's face is a direct sign of his character, and that White describes his mouth, even in a letter, by a trope that stretches visualisation to its limits, because its motivation is thematic. Being 'like a piece of fence-wire' points to Voss's tensions and his masculine capacity to make distinctions rather than to the contours of the human mouth.

More to the point, though, as we began to see in analysing White's Australia, his characters come in two main kinds: those who have an interiority deep or rich enough to be capable of destruction and fragmentation and those who do not. The second kind tend to be described as 'types', a tendency of which White was very aware: we recall, for instance, his worry that his Australian characters were too stereotypical. For that reason, these characters do not just belong to a single novel: they form a system of repetitions and differences across the novels. The same 'character' appears with variations in novel after novel, being used not to push forward an individual novel's grand 'theme' but White's overarching cultural critique (to the extent that these levels can be distinguished).

Take, for instance, White's beautiful women, what we can call the 'Madeleine type' after the first such character in *The Tree of Man*, whose most fully realised instance is Boo Hollingrake/Olivia Davenport in *The Vivisector*. They are characteristically seen from afar, objects of desire, embodiments of class and glamour. The closer the narration comes to them, the less substance they have. It is as if they are held together by narcissism, symbolised by Mrs Hunter's looking-glass, which has been the pivot of her life but which, in old age, she can hardly see. They become objects of desire precisely because they are never completely present to themselves or others: they exist in their appearance and style, even despite themselves. It is a little reductive to talk of them as theatrical, because to be theatrical means to act out a role, whereas these characters do not so much act roles as project themselves. They are stars. Because they have so little essence they are uncontainable: no relationship, no house, no social identity can hold them. Those who desire them can never become intimate with them: there is not enough selfhood there for intimacy. Because they remain remote, they are capable of treachery and abandonment. In one of the most powerful instances, from *The Eye of the Storm*, the glamorous Sister Manhood abandons her drunken lesbian cousin in a pub, which is not just a sign of her moral superficiality but, at a meta-level, a punishment for her own heterosexual attractiveness. Yet, given White's judgements on what constitutes good ways of living and being, these characters have quite a specific value. Unlike his really evil characters, they are not imprisoned in pettiness and conventionality, nor are they malevolent (they do not feel hard done by). Unlike his passively good characters, they are not dependent on their own generosity and hence on other people's selfishness or failure. Yet, unlike his most privileged characters (born male), they cannot act on the world: they remain more powerful for others than for themselves.

Set against the beautiful are what we can call White's bimbos. They belong to a realm of popular misogyny, combining something of the 'fat and fair' characters of Victorian fiction with the more open sexuality of the kind of woman Marilyn Monroe played (and parodied) in the movies. White's bimbos are heart-breakers and narcissists; they are dumb and age badly, ending up in mindless, usually dissatisfied, maternity and domesticity. But they are more dangerous than the popular-cultural version of the type. Deep down, they have a latent cruelty. A good example of the type is Belle Bonner of *Voss*, the pretty, conventional daughter of Voss's patrons. Here she is farewelling Voss's party:

> 'You may send me a black's spear,' she called, and laughed, 'with blood on it.'
>
> Her lips were young and red. Her own blood raced. Her thoughts moved in pictures. (*Voss* 116)

The idea of a spear, red (like Belle's lips) with an Aborigine's blood, is not just stupid and insensitive, it is sadistic. But it is not simply her own private idea: 'Her thoughts moved in pictures' places Belle's bloodthirstiness in a wider context. It belongs to a mind like a movie (just as she has a 'starlet's' body). For White, the bimbo, particularly the ageing bimbo, often thinks the thoughts and feels the passions of the community as a whole, but only the least sensitive thoughts and passions.

Thus it is, for instance, that the notion of lynching Himmelfarb in *Riders in the Chariot* is first conceived by Mrs Jolley and Mrs Flack, two scheming, dissatisfied women who have become total life-deniers. Indeed these characters were broadly modelled from newspaper stories of real-life murderers. As a type the life-denier is petit-bourgeois: Sister

Badgery in *The Eye of the Storm*, the choric women at the beginning and end of *A Fringe of Leaves*, characters like Miss Docker of 'A Cheery Soul'. It is not just that they possess zero-degree interiority, they lack the multiple package of identities that White ascribed to himself and characters like Hurtle. In fact they express without qualification society's fear of fragmentation, dissidence and transgression, a fear that leads them straight to hypocrisy, and to scapegoating the weak, the different or those with more complex subjectivities.

The bimbo, in turn, contrasts with the trusting women of White's fictions — Elsie in *The Tree of Man*, or Connie in *The Living and the Dead* — women who love their men without reservation, who are integrated and have integrity, among them the good servant type discussed in chapter 2. In the end, these characters' integrity fails because it provides no room for transgressive desire and, once more, the saving 'disease' of being 'many in one'. Their wholeness stands in the way of the capacity to imagine, to suffer, to sympathise. But, more complexly, in these characters I think we confront most forthrightly the difficulties that White had in imagining female desire in general. He may have thought that he too was a woman, sometimes beautiful, sometimes maybe even trusting, sometimes desirable, but as a woman he was an object not a subject of desire.

Perhaps for that reason, White's male characters are less typified. There is, however, one major exception, a type who does appear more than once — the tearaway — who, as I have already argued, expresses a particularly colonial relation between community and family life. The best instance is Ray, the bad son who ends up a rootless petty criminal in *The Tree of Man*. Garnet Roxburgh in *A Fringe of Leaves* is another example with a major narrative role. These are characters who flee domesticity and family life; unable to settle, they have no ties to place; unable to join communities, they have no values. They are unscrupulous, uncaring of the pain they cause others. And, like Roxburgh, with his 'coarse and sensual' presence, they exude heterosexuality (*FL* 83).

It is a particularly fascinating type, because here White comes closest to imagining 'otherness'. These characters are further from White's idea of himself than his women characters are. And yet it seems that, as far as White was concerned, a genius has a bit of this character in him too. Hurtle, for instance, is not completely disconnected from Ray, the key to the connection being precisely that capacity to hurt other people, to drop them, in the effort not to be entrapped by the heterosexual family and relationships. Artists are transgressive, they live beyond relationships — that is what makes the artist too a kind of tearaway. The crucial difference between the artist-tearaway and the criminal-tearaway in White seems to be that the first are queer and the second are straight, which in this instance is more an expression of an autobiographical aesthetic than anything else, including a politics.

Closure

Let us end with White's endings. He has two main ways of closing his stories: by returning to the beginning in a circular movement, as in *The Tree of Man*, or by delivering the narrative up to fragmentation as in *The Vivisector* and *The Aunt's Story*. *The Tree of Man* ends, like Hardy's *Jude the Obscure*, with a member of the next generation beginning the story again, but this time, sentimentally, the boy is a would-be poet burning to write the 'poem of life' that his grandfather and father could never record. (Waldo Brown of *The Solid Mandala* is this little boy grown up and turning out a failure; Hurtle of *The Vivisector* is this little boy grown up to be a success.) Because of this circular ending, *The Tree of Man* can close, sententiously, with the words 'in the end, there was no end'. It was the second time that White had used this technique: *The Living and the Dead*, which has a more sophisticated temporal structure than any of the other novels, ends exactly where it began, with Elyot Standish seeing his sister Eden off at a railway station after his old nurse Julia has departed, heroically, for the Spanish Civil War. Within this tight cyclical structure, the main body of the novel, which tells the story of the Standish family and focuses on the closeted homosexual Elyot's aimlessness, seems to lead nowhere.

This circular closure is used most subtly in *The Eye of the Storm*, in an ending that fleshes out a somewhat similar final scene in *Riders in the Chariot*. Here the night nurse, Sister de Santis, finds herself in Mrs Hunter's room at sunrise, after the latter's death. Sister de Santis is the novel's holy person, like Mrs Godbold of *Riders in the Chariot*, a servant drawn to redemption 'as clear as morning light' (12), which she finds in nursing's asceticism, discipline and proximity to death. In the novel's final words, she bows her head 'amazed and not a little frightened by what she saw in Elizabeth Hunter's looking glass'. What does she see? Two things: first, a dead body — that of Mrs Lippman, the Jewish refugee and housekeeper, who has just committed suicide after a lifetime of xenophobic persecution; second, the sight of her own beatitude — 'The light she could not ward off: it was by now too solid, too possessive; herself possessed'. This gaze refers back to the novel's first scene, in which the dying, almost blind, ex-beauty Mrs Hunter wakes up being attended to by Sister de Santis and believes it will be a good day because, for once, she can see herself in the mirror. Mrs Lippman's death is the obverse of Mrs Hunter's failing narcissism; it is a sacrifice that keeps the Hunters' world going. But the loop between the novel's first and last scenes does not point to a dead-end, as it did in *The Living and the Dead*. Rather, it celebrates the power of light, and expands the scene's textual connotations (just because the end refers back to the beginning). Against the odds, and at the very end, the novel affirms Mrs Hunter's youthful good looks *and* Mrs Lippman's tragic end *and* Sister de Santis's austere beatitude. No char-acter, not even Sister de Santis, can accept the glory of a murderous world in the way that, for a moment, guided by the text, the reader can. It is a ploy that risks complacency, simply confirming the sunny side of the genius's insights into human tragedy, but maybe it comes off here because the narrative structure is doing the signifying work rather than the narrative voice. This time, the message is communicat-ed without sententious declaration, and the text achieves a powerful moral (rather than spiritual) effect without drawing on the writer's personal experience or wisdom.

* * *

I began by claiming that White's work needs to be read in the light of the tensions between his theatricality and his spirituality. After analysing the social and cultural contexts in which he wrote, made a career, and formed his public and private identities, I have ended by suggesting that his narratives should be read in terms of the tension between their sym-bolism and what I called his autobiographical aesthetic — his living for and in his writing. What is the connection between these two 'tensions'?

Quite a simple one, I would suggest. White's symbolism *is* his spiritualism expressed in the medium of fictional narrative, just as his autobiographical aesthetic is a means through which he could use novel-writing to present himself to the public in many roles — as if on a stage. But, as we have seen, by turning to fiction, White could only affirm the life of spirit by hinting at that life's hollowness. Likewise, by using his novels (partly) to project himself he reduced his internal theatre, his being 'many in one', into the promotion of himself as a genius. This kind of reading, clearly, makes White a more empty writer than he has previously been considered.

I have also argued that White was a powerful cultural critic. This too limits him, not least because his Australia, especially in its conceptions of suburbia, Aborigines, women and homosexuality, does not quite fit the Australia of the 1990s. We can draw these two threads of my argument together by recognising that, if White is going to have a strong place in a future Australian national culture, it is not as a writer who transcended the prejudices of his time (and class and education and so on) through his spirituality and genius, but as one who lived and wrote and fought those prejudices intensely and tensely enough to keep them vital.

This leaves us with a number of paradoxes, two of which need to be emphasised. In the period during which he became famous, White reconciled himself to Australia by attempting to supply the national culture with regenerative myths based on the idea of sacrifice. Those hard-working, ascetic loners, Stan, Voss and Himmelfarb, versions of White himself, are, in their various ways, all sacrificed for their ideals. White's imagining their (fictional) lives is supposed to bind passion, meaning and memories to the country. But, as I have argued, White is involved in making sacrifices of his own, which work according to another, invisible system of values. What White is ridiculing, damning, black-magicking away is, most of all, the Australian ordinariness of his time. The problem with saying this, however, is that that ordinariness was itself a myth, as became clearer during the 1960s when differences within the 'ordinary' — differences of ethnicity, gender, sexuality, generation and so on — were slowly recognised. I would argue that it is because Australian 'ordinariness' was indeed a dangerous myth that certain readers could accept White's self-aggrandising fiction-myths of sacrifice so willingly. It follows that his extraordinary status in the national culture will be maintained so long as the country needs critiques of ordinariness and his readers can overlook how, in his novels, the primary figure of that ordinariness and the object of his exorcisms is, again and again, the middle-aged, middle-class, not highly educated, suburban woman.

My feeling is that, given this, White's critique of Australian ordinariness is no longer especially vital or useful, and that his reputation as Australia's *genius loci* means that it is more important to criticise than to join him. He is doomed to be increasingly neglected, or, at any rate, celebrated only in lip-service. With one qualification. Paradoxically, his work stands against what have become the dominant *institutions* of the cultural nationalism whose icon he is. Everything that he wrote implicitly rebuked official culture, that is, culture as viewed from the state's point of view as a national resource to be administered and taught. Of course, today, official Australian culture is characterised by a policy of tolerance and integration. It is a tolerance that is softly repressive though: where is scandalous, difficult, truly heterodox writing and culture being produced or sought after? In part, it is this tolerance that has allowed White — that queer, largely Australia-hating writer — to become the icon he is. None the less, from the official point of view, there remains a more deeply heterodox White. After all, it is hard to tolerate the White that I have criticised: the elitist White, the White who fictionalised contemporary Aboriginal life away, the misogynist White, the White who affirmed incest, even the White who thought of himself as a genius because he was psychically sick or damaged, and the (intimately related) White who considered art and literature as too profound to be simply available as an administrative and educational resource. These aspects of White I find it hard to accept too. But just because they do not help produce good citizens or a good society (as official policies and most of us currently picture them), they might outlast the kind of criticism I have outlined in this book and disprove my confidence that White's writings will not be valued as highly in the future as they have been in the past.

NOTES

The career

1 John Curtain, 'Book publishing', in *The Media in Australia: Industries, Texts, Audiences,* ed. Stuart Cunningham and Graeme Turner (Sydney: Allen & Unwin, 1993), 110.

2 Alan Lawson, 'Unmerciful dingoes? The Critical Reception of Patrick White', *Meanjin* 32 (1973), 379–92.

3 R. F. Brissenden, 'Patrick White', *Meanjin* 18 (1959), 419.

4 See the advertisement for the anthology in *Meanjin* 15 (1956), 225.

The Australian

1 Cited in Tim Rowse, *Australian Liberalism and National Character* (Malmsbury: Kibble Books, 1978), 117.

2 K. S. Prichard, 'Comment', *Overland* 13 (1958), 14.

3 Geoffrey Bolton, *The Oxford History of Australia, vol 5, 1942–1988: The Middle Way* (Melbourne: Oxford University Press, 1990), 122.

4 Harry Heseltine, 'The Literary Heritage', in *On Native Grounds*, ed. C. B. Christesen (Sydney: Angus & Robertson, 1968), 15; A. A. Phillips, *The Australian Tradition* (Melbourne: Cheshire, 1958), 44.

5 Thelma Herring and G. A. Wilkes, 'A Conversation with Patrick White', in *Days of Wine and Roses*, ed. Frank Moorhouse (Ringwood: Penguin, 1980), 190.

6 Robin Boyd, *Australia's Home* (Ringwood: Penguin, 1968), 258.

7 Roger Callois, 'Festival', in *The College of Sociology*, ed. Denis Hollier (Minneapolis: University of Minnesota Press, 1988), 294.

The cultural critic

1 Douglas W. Druick, *Odilon Redon: Prince of Dreams* (Chicago: Art Institute of Chicago, 1994), 332–3.

Sex and the family

1 See Judith Butler, *Bodies that Matter: On the Discursive Limits of 'Sex'* (New York: Routledge, 1983), 255–6, who thinks about mothers in terms somewhat like these.

2 See Michel Foucault, *A History of Sexuality: Volume 1, An Introduction*, trans. Robert Hurley (New York: Vintage, 1980), for the classic articulation of this argument.

3 Theodor Adorno, *Aesthetic Theory*, trans. C. Lenhardt, ed. Gretel Adorno and Rolf Tiedemann (London: Routledge and Kegan Paul, 1984), 116. For Benjamin's similar point see John McCole, *Walter Benjamin and the Antinomies of Tradition* (Ithaca, NY: Cornell University Press, 1993), 121.

4 Eve Sedgwick, *Epistemology of the Closet* (Berkeley: University of California Press, 1990), 165.

Narrative techniques

1 Cited in Jacqueline Chéneiux-Gendron, *Surrealism* (New York: Columbia University Press, 1990), 181.

2 André Breton, *Manifestoes of Surrealism* (Ann Arbor: University of Michigan Press, 1972), 36.

BIBLIOGRAPHY

PRIMARY SOURCES

Novels

The Aunt's Story (Harmondsworth: Penguin, 1969). First published 1948.

The Eye of the Storm (Harmondsworth: Penguin, 1975). First published 1973.

A Fringe of Leaves (London: Jonathan Cape, 1976).

Happy Valley (London: George Harrap, 1939).

The Living and the Dead (Harmondsworth: Penguin, 1967). First published 1941.

Memoirs of Many in One (London: Jonathan Cape 1986).

Riders in the Chariot (Harmondsworth: Penguin, 1964). First published 1961.

The Solid Mandala (Harmondsworth: Penguin, 1969). First published 1966.

The Tree of Man (Harmondsworth: Penguin, 1961). First published 1955.

The Twyborn Affair (London: Jonathan Cape, 1979).

The Vivisector (Harmondsworth: Penguin, 1973). First published 1970.

Voss (Harmondsworth: Penguin, 1960). First published 1957.

Short Stories

The Burnt Ones (Harmondsworth: Penguin, 1968). First published 1964.

The Cockatoos (Harmondsworth: Penguin, 1978). First published 1974.

The Night the Prowler: Short Story and Screenplay (Harmondsworth: Penguin, 1978).
Three Uneasy Pieces (Melbourne: Pascoe, 1987).

Plays
Big Toys (Sydney: Currency Press, 1978).
Four Plays (Melbourne: Sun Books, 1967). First published 1965.
Netherwood (Sydney: Currency Press, 1983).
Signal Driver (Sydney: Currency Press, 1983).

Poems
The Ploughman and Other Poems (Sydney: Beacon Press, 1935).
Thirteen Poems (Sydney: private, n.d.)

Nonfiction
Flaws in the Glass: A Self-Portrait (London: Penguin, 1983). First published 1981.
Herring, Thelma and G. A. Wilkes, 'A Conversation with Patrick White', in *Days of Wine and Roses*, ed. Frank Moorhouse (Ringwood: Penguin, 1980), 188–98. First published in *Southerly* 1973.
Letters, ed. David Marr (Sydney: Random House, 1994).
Patrick White Speaks, ed. Paul Brennan and Christine Flynn (Sydney: Primavera Press, 1989).

SECONDARY SOURCES
White criticism
Akerholt, May-Brit, *Patrick White* (Amsterdam: Rodolphi, 1988).
Argyle, Barry, *Patrick White* (Edinburgh and London: Oliver and Boyd, 1967).
Beatson, Peter, *The Eye in the Mandala: Patrick White: a vision of man and god* (Sydney: Reed, 1977).
Bliss, Carolyn, *Patrick White's Fiction: the paradox of fortunate failure* (New York: St Martin's Press, 1986).
Brissenden, R.F., 'Patrick White', *Meanjin* 18 (1959), 411–25.

Dutton, Geoffrey, *Patrick White* (Melbourne: Oxford University Press, 1971).

Edgecombe, Rodney Stenning, *Vision and Style in Patrick White* (Tuscaloosa and London: University of Alabama Press, 1989).

Hansson, Karin, *The Warped Universe: a study of imagery and structure in seven novels by Patrick White* (Lund: CWK Gleerup, 1984).

Kiernan, Brian, *Patrick White* (London: Macmillan, 1980).

Lawson, Alan, 'Unmerciful Dingoes? The critical reception of Patrick White', *Meanjin* 32 (1973), 379–92.

McCulloch, A.M., *A Tragic Vision: the novels of Patrick White* (St Lucia: University of Queensland Press, 1983).

Marr, David, *Patrick White: A Life* (Sydney: Random House, 1991).

Morley, Patricia A., *The mystery of unity: themes and techniques in the novels of Patrick White* (St Lucia: University of Queensland Press, 1972).

Tacey, David, *Patrick White: Fiction and the Unconscious* (Melbourne: Oxford University Press, 1988).

Walsh, William, *Patrick White's Fiction* (Sydney: Allen & Unwin, 1977).

Williams, Mark, *Patrick White* (Basingstoke: Macmillan, 1993).

Wolfe, Peter, *Laden Choirs: the fiction of Patrick White* (Lexington: University of Kentucky, 1983).

GENERAL CRITICISM AND CONTEXT

Adorno, T.W., *Aesthetic Theory*, ed. Gretel Adorno and Rolf Tiedemann, trans. C. Lenhardt (London: Routledge & Kegan Paul, 1984).

Bolton, Geoffrey, *The Oxford History of Australia, vol. 5, 1942–1988: The Middle Way* (Melbourne: Oxford University Press, 1990).

Boyd, Robin, *Australia's Home* (Ringwood: Penguin, 1968).

Breton, André, *Manifestoes of Surrealism*, trans. Richard Seaver and Helen R. Lane (Ann Arbor: University of Michigan Press, 1972).

Butler, Judith, *Bodies that Matter: On the Discursive Limits of 'Sex'* (New York: Routledge, 1993).

Callois, Roger, 'Festival', in *The College of Sociology*, ed. Denis Hollier (Minneapolis: University of Minnesota Press, 1988), 279–304.

Chéneiux-Gendron, Jacqueline, *Surrealism* (New York: Columbia University Press, 1990).

Curtain, John, 'Book publishing', in *The Media in Australia: Industries, Texts, Audiences*, ed. Stuart Cunningham and Graeme Turner (Sydney: Allen & Unwin, 1993), 102–18.

Docker, John, *Australian Cultural Elites: Intellectual Traditions in Sydney and Melbourne* (Sydney: Angus & Robertson, 1974).

Druick, Douglas W., *Odilon Redon: Prince of Dreams* (Chicago: Art Institute of Chicago, 1994).

Foucault, Michel, *A History of Sexuality: vol. 1, An Introduction*, trans. Robert Hurley (New York: Vintage, 1980).

Gibson, Ross, *South of the West: Postcolonialism and the narrative construction of Australia* (Bloomington: Indiana University Press, 1992).

Heseltine, Harry, 'The Literary Heritage', in *On Native Grounds*, ed. C. B. Christesen (Sydney: Angus & Robertson, 1968), 3–15.

Hodge, Bob and Vijay Mishra, *The Dark Side of the Dream: Australian Literature and the Postcolonial Mind* (Sydney: Allen & Unwin, 1991).

Lees, Stella and June Senyard, *The Fifties* (Melbourne: Hyland House, 1987).

McCole, John, *Walter Benjamin and the Antinomies of Tradition* (Ithaca: Cornell University Press, 1993).

Miller, D.A., *The Novel and the Police* (Berkeley: University of California Press, 1988).

Philips, A.A., *The Australian Tradition* (Melbourne: Cheshire, 1958).

Prichard, K.S., 'Comment', *Overland* 13 (1958), 14.

Rowse, Tim, *Australian Liberalism and National Character* (Malmsbury: Kibble Books, 1978).

Sedgwick, Eve Kosofsky, *Epistemology of the Closet* (Berkeley: University of California Press, 1990).

Sedgwick, Eve Kosofsky, *Tendencies* (Durham: Duke University Press, 1993).

Wilkes, G.A., *The Stockyard and the Croquet Lawn: Literary Evidence of Australia's Cultural Development* (Sydney: Edward Arnold, 1981).